AN OBJECT OF GRAC

An Object of Grace and Love

LIN HEPING
(MOTHER OF WATCHMAN NEE)

Written in 1943
(translated by Miss Hilda Holms)

KINGSWAY PUBLICATIONS
EASTBOURNE

First published 1943 in Chinese by the Shanghai Book Room
First published in English by Kingsway 2006

Design for cover by CCD (www.ccdgroup.co.uk)

ISBN: 1 84291 266 6
ISBN: 978–1–842912–66–9

KINGSWAY COMMUNICATIONS LTD
Lottbridge Drove, Eastbourne BN23 6NT, England.
Email: books@kingsway.co.uk
Printed in the USA

Preface

This is the autobiography of a Chinese woman born in 1880 who lived mainly in sea ports along the coastline of south eastern China. It makes not only fascinating reading but also tells of the spiritually challenging experiences of the writer from which so much can be learned.

Lin Heping was born into a poverty stricken home with parents who felt they could not support yet another child, let alone a girl. They therefore arranged her adoption by the childless concubine of a wealthy businessman. When she was found to be a lively, attractive and unusually bright child, she was given an education not often available to girls. On completing her secondary school studies, she was sent to Shanghai to improve her English with a view to admission to an American university to study medicine.

All her cherished career ambitions were thwarted, however, when her 'mother' realised that there were likely to be long periods of separation and so swiftly arranged a marriage for her. She became Mrs Ni, wife of a customs officer from a nominally Christian home, and with him parented nine children.

Even these responsibilities were not sufficient for such a strong-willed and self-sufficient temperament, and she took part in the revolutionary politics at a time when Communist Mao was invading from the north to oust democratic Sun Yat Sen (whom she faithfully supported) from power. Later she became a member of the local ladies' club where gambling and mah-jong were the obsession.

Quite suddenly and dramatically this was followed by her conversion to Christianity and her devoted following of the Lord Jesus whom she recognised as her Saviour. It so happened that her eldest son, her third child, known later as Watchman Nee, had the same experience very shortly afterwards and often after this their lives were linked in joint service to God.

Her son's story is told in *Against the Tide*, a biography written by Angus Kinnear. While he was compiling his book he found the mother's autobiography in Chinese amongst some papers. He was able to use some information from it when Miss Hilda Holms, a retired missionary, graciously offered to translate it for him. So this book is her translation from the original Chinese into English, retaining as far as possible Lin Heping's own style of writing and words.

Mrs Ni's autobiography closes in 1943. She died in 1950. Two years later her son Watchman was arrested and in 1956 imprisoned with a twenty-year sentence for his faith in Jesus Christ.

Though we may choose to disagree with some of her

views formed through the culture and teaching of the time, the lessons she learned during her long life of faith and service to God are for us all – as are the joys of knowing His loving care and patience surrounding us.

Jean Kinnear, 2006

Chapter 1

God most high, most hallowed, who can tell Your grace? Is it not those who have received grace themselves? But as Your grace is so great and deep towards this reprobate, how can I tell it? Oh my God, You only are Lord. Those whom You want to speak must obey without questioning. My God, I praise You because Your grace and mercy are shown towards a chief of sinners like me, that men might know You love great sinners and cause them to come before You, to come near to You, to obtain Your mercy and grace. Therefore, trusting Your grace, I dare to take up my pen and write what You want me to.

*   *   *

I was born into a poor family in 1880. Because living was hard for my own family, and because there was an evil custom of esteeming boys and despising girls, I was sent to a rich man as a servant. At that time it happened that there was a merchant's concubine who wanted to adopt a girl as a daughter. As soon as a go-between was invited to make the negotiations, it was accomplished. Oh God, I cannot but praise and thank You as I see You act in this! The Bible says, 'I will have mercy on whom I have mercy, and I will have compassion on whom I have compassion' (Romans 9:15). You separated me from my mother's womb and by grace are my God. I worship You!

When I came to the merchant's home, they really loved and wanted children, and in a short time I was lively and loveable. So I became like a pearl in their palm, the love of their hearts and truly their daughter, and they became my cherished and respected parents. My parents' love to me increased with the days, even to our mutual dependence for life. My smiles and tears touched their hearts. Oh, this is wonderful! My own parents could discard me,[1] but my parents who brought me up loved me as their life. Oh God, I say Your grace treated me graciously.

When I was six years old my mother bound my feet, so that I should be good looking. During this year my father suddenly became seriously ill. It was a strange illness – all the doctors were helpless and did not know what to do. Just when we got to the point of no return, the manager of my father's firm (the Fu Le Yang Company), Mr Zhang, who was a member of the Methodist church and loved the Lord very much, mentioned asking the pastor to pray. My parents only sought healing through the usual channels, but as the manager proposed it, who could say anything about how it was done? The merciful God at that time heard the pastor's prayer and healed my father without medicine. From this time the holy name of the Lord Jesus entered the ears of our family, and within several days we cast away all

---

[1] Literally 'throw me away'.

the idols from our home, and even my bound feet were released. The whole family believed in the Lord Jesus, entered the church and were baptised. My father followed his manager, Mr Zhang, to the Methodist church for baptism because it was near his firm, and my mother and I went to the Anglican church for baptism because it was near our home. When I was baptised, cold water was reverently rubbed on my head and the pastor read a few sentences of Scripture about the truth of baptism, all very mysterious.

After this my parents sent me to a private country school near where we lived. Every Sunday I went with my mother to worship, and from Mr Lin's mother I learned many scriptures and could sing several hymns. In noonday leisure time at school I was once unconsciously singing hymns, and the teacher heard and called me before him to give our testimony – how my father was healed, how the family cast away idols, how we were baptised and entered the church, etc. Truly God, who is merciful to men, spoke His wonders through the mouth of a child. The teacher was very happy to hear this, and the next Sunday he and his wife and mother went with this recipient-of-grace child and my mother to worship. Later their whole family believed in the Lord Jesus as their Saviour, were baptised and entered the church, just as our family did.

From this time I was not only my parents' lively treasure at home, but at school I was also the lively treasure of the teacher, his wife and aged mother. When they had something nice to eat they always left some for me, though they feared I might not eat it as my home was better off than theirs. But my mother also remembered their poverty and often sent many things to them through me, as we went back and forth in increasing intimacy. On the day that Miss Lo, of the Church of England, and my teacher's family were baptised, there was unspeakable joy and praise as they said, 'We truly thank our heavenly Father, true God, that a little girl has led us to belong to the Lord.' When I heard this, I took no notice; it was as though God had done it, not I.

Soon my parents increased in fervour, and heard that in the country there was a primary Christian school opened by a foreign businessman (of Dian Fu Yang Company). They decided to send me there. All the books were taught by church pastors and notables, using Fuzhou dialect, usually with two examinations a year. If the examinations were done well there were scholarships. Although my family had money for me, actually it was better for me to use money gained from working at my studies: it gave a little more 'face'.

When I was eleven years old, a teacher called Mr Li exhorted my father to send me to an eminent Methodist mission girls' school to study for my betterment. My father not only loved me, he was a reasonable man who, hearing this, did accordingly. My father's first wife had two boys and one girl, and he decided to send the two boys to an English-Chinese college founded by Mr Zhang, and he sent me to the eminent girls' school in the country. When I entered the school, the first person I came in contact with was an American, Miss Bonafield. My first teacher was Miss Xi. She was a good teacher in needlework, cooking, purity, hygiene – everything was very good. Every Saturday she took me home, because it was near where we lived, thus teachers and pupils regarded me as more favoured than others.

Before long I moved up a class and was instructed by

another teacher, Miss Huang. She was a particularly good teacher. She understood English well; her speech and deportment were refined; she was lovable. Although I was young, I had a clear perception of people's dispositions, and I was fully satisfied to have such a person as my teacher. So I was particularly careful and increasingly liked the subjects she taught, and I was top of the whole class every time. Because of this she especially regarded me, and wanted me to sit in the front. Seeing that I could explain the lesson, she always nodded as though I was the most satisfying pupil in the whole class.

Then one day after lunch a pupil asked me to play tennis, and I forgot that I had study to do and said I would go. Just at the height of the game the school bell sounded and we set off to the class taught by my dear teacher. Then I remembered that I had not properly prepared my lesson and was thoroughly grieved. Tears fell, and I did not know what to do. I went to the classroom, sat in the front, did not say a word, and did not stop crying. That day I not only displeased my teacher who loved me, but I surprised her very much. Seeing these circumstances she asked me why I was crying. At first I did not answer. 'Are you ill?' she asked. I shook my head. 'Has somebody taken advantage of you?' I stood on my feet and said, 'I will tell you later,' crying as I spoke. She nodded and allowed me to sit down. Oh, what compassion! According to custom, if you could not remember the lesson you could not sit down – you had to stand until the lesson was over.

After school, like a compassionate mother, she nodded to me, took me to her room and asked, 'Whatever has happened today?'

I said, 'I am not sick, and nobody has taken advantage of me. I myself am naughty, I forgot to do my homework and went to play tennis, then the bell rang and I remembered but it was too late to prepare.' I asked her to forgive me, and said I was grateful she had not made me stand before everybody until the end of the lesson.

The more I said, the more I wept, and my incomparable repentance touched her heart. She left her seat, gave me two big oranges and told me not to cry. She liked me speaking like this. Seeing that she treated me thus, I was both ashamed and grateful, for I had wept bitterly. She also gave me a very pretty scent bottle and spoke many comforting and loving words, which sent me away with no more tears. When I came out of the teacher's room there were several pupils waiting outside the door wanting to know how she had treated me, and they were truly amazed to see two big oranges and a pretty scent bottle in my hands. I was most grateful to that teacher who treated me graciously, and I told several people of her compassionate dealing.

Now let us think of our God. When we sin, we only need to be willing to come before Him and truthfully speak the circumstances and ask Him to forgive, and He will not only forgive our sin, but will give us His Son, the Lord Jesus Christ, to be our Saviour, our life and our all. Oh, how great is His compassion and mercy! I wish many more people would come and receive His grace and blessing. Now I also know that my dear teacher is one who knows Christ. How do I know? When I was at school at Christmas a foreign friend of hers who was a musician asked her to compose a Chinese hymn. We had the tune, but regretfully no words. Then my teacher wrote the following words:

> The Saviour is the true God,
> He became flesh, came down in mortal life,
> Gave Himself as man to a virgin's womb;
> Died in place of men to forgive sin, save souls.

On Christmas evening she, together with several teachers who loved the Lord, sang it three or four times. I was amazed, and because it was composed by my teacher I learnt it and sang it vigorously until I could repeat and sing it. At Christmas this teacher also composed another hymn:

> Which day is today?
> The day the Saviour came down and was born.
> The Saviour was born today.
> Everybody praise Him.
> Child of the manger;
> Christ's King of Peace,
> All princes come, kneel in worship.
> What brightness of Glory!
> Hallelujah, Glory, Amen.

From these two hymns it was evident that my teacher knew the Lord Christ. Praise the Lord, today I also am one who knows the Lord Jesus Christ. Oh, what wonderful grace this is! Even the chief of sinners has a share in His grace. May worship, glory and thanksgiving be to the Lord Jesus for ever. Amen.

Our principal was an American who truly loved the Lord. Every Sunday she took us to church to worship. Once aged Pastor Hwa had revival meetings, I also took part and wept. I saw I needed a Saviour, and knew my sins were many and the Saviour was willing to forgive me, but I did not yet know that because of this I could escape perdition and have eternal life. So when I sinned I feared being cast into hell. When I first perceived the Lord's love, I thought that going to heaven or hell was a matter of our deeds, so that all the time heaven or hell was uncertain. Sometimes I was keen, but gradually it came to nothing. Thank God, I now know that our salvation is entirely due to the Lord Jesus dying and shedding His blood in our stead. He died in our stead – we escape death. How trustworthy! Heaven and earth can change, but the word of the Lord is settled in heaven for ever more. If God says those who believe have eternal life, then they have eternal life.

When I was sixteen years old I asked my principal to write a letter to America to negotiate for me to go there and study medicine. Before long there was a reply saying they were willing, subject to results. With impetuosity I then proposed to my father that before I went to America it was necessary first to go to Shanghai to study English, lest when I got there I had the difficulty of not understanding the language. My father responded immediately with approval. When I was seventeen it happened that Pastor Li's daughter also wanted to go to America to study medicine, so I immediately determined to go together with her on the boat to the Shanghai Chinese-Western Girls' School to study.

This was the first time I had left Fuzhou. Arriving at Shanghai, I found the place and people were strange; their speech was not the same, and I tasted homesickness. But because I urgently wanted to study, I had to endure it. Within a few days a letter came from home saying that because I had come to Shanghai to study, and because she had heard that I was going to America to study medicine, my mother, an elderly lady, was weeping and unable to eat.

Later a friend of my father was asked to exhort me to return home, so my mother would be willing to diminish her fast. At that time I read the letter carefully and wept much, but soon thoughts of home gradually receded in my mind. I studied all the more, and spent the time solely on my lessons. I remember I had only been in the school three weeks when I finished the first English document, and knew it well, so my teacher put me on the second book. Moreover, in the examination my name came out first.

From this time I lifted my head up in pride and paid attention to fashions in dress. Besides the school fees, every month my father gave me ten dollars' pocket money; my older brother gave me two dollars, and my second brother gave me five dollars. Although I had seventeen dollars a month, it still was not enough. Because of this I began to sin, and appropriated my monthly five-dollar music fee for my own use. I did not learn to play, but after school I taught myself, not receiving instruction from my teacher. So I had a few more dollars each month to spend.

After all, man's desires are a bottomless pit, and I devised another plan. I asked my parents on their birthdays, because I could not be at home to enjoy the happiness and was alone away, to send me a little more money, so that being away from the family I might still have enjoyment. With these kinds of words coming to their ears, both parents could not but send me money. They were also religious people, and at Christmas, Easter and the New Year especially remembered me and sent money for me to spend. Thus in a year I added several tens of dollars for pocket money, and was a perfect deceiver.

Our principal, Miss Haygood, was a keen religious person.

She saw I studied well, and really liked me very much. At the same time, because I had influence on others but was unconcerned as to religion, she came to me one day and said, 'Come to my room at 4.30 p.m. today.' I said, 'Yes,' but my heart was beating as I did not know whether it was for good or ill. At 4.30 I went to her study. She asked me to sit down, then prayed. Then she began to talk about religious matters, and mentioned my proud influence, etc. I listened, but was unaffected, though troubled. I thought she should just want me not to break the school rules, study well and be a good student, and as for the rest – what had she to do with it? Although she disapproved of me, actually among the teachers and pupils I had a little favour.

She settled that every Wednesday at 4 p.m. I was to go and see her. She meant it in a kind way, but on my part I really felt this was annoying! But I had no way to escape and could only answer, 'I will come.' When she spoke to me she spoke in English, not in Shanghai dialect, taking it that as I was a Fuzhou person come to Shanghai, I did not understand Shanghai dialect – but in fact I knew it before I came there. Nonetheless, I profited by this time in learning a lot more English so that I could display my ability before my classmates and get glory for myself. Oh my God, I truly acknowledge I am a most wicked and chief of sinners, taking Your grace to be my own wisdom and talent. Although it is so, oh my God, where sin abounded, grace did much more abound.

When I was eighteen years old, my mother was still afraid I would go abroad to study medicine and not come home. Being uneasy about me day and night, she vexedly arranged a marriage for me. It happened that the wife of

Pastor Ni Yucheng sent a man forward to seek a wife for her son, Mr Ni Wenxiu. This was in agreement with my mother's heart. After the inquiries were suitably completed, the old lady went away with great rejoicing. My father's heart was betwixt agreeing and not agreeing. He was not sanguine about my mother's pressure, but could only acquiesce.

They wrote a letter to inform me. As I held it up and read it, it was as though there was a crash of thunder. My ambition had come to nothing. I could only return home under sufferance. I had no alternative. (At that time girls were timid, and their marriages were entirely settled by their parents.) When I arrived home my parents gave me Mr Ni's photograph. After this, although I did not say a word, within me was born a hatred of my mother. I regarded her as one who had ruined my future.

During some months at home my parents were incomparably busy preparing for my wedding, and my heart was incomparably cold. I knew that useless girls planned to get married, but others could be independent and become teachers, doctors and important people. Me? Finished – go and get married! Truly I was crestfallen. Before long my fiancé wrote to me saying the marriage was defined by heaven. Although he had many girls spoken of for marriage, no arrangement had been completed with them, but finally he rejoiced that as soon as I was mentioned it was settled, and he was very happy. He also said that he had seen me when I was in Fujian. But I never knew him. In the letter he specially said he wanted me to reply. Oh dear Lord, how hard it was for a girl unwilling to be married to write to a man she had never met! After a few days I could not help but write an indifferent letter in reply. In these few months he often wrote to me.

We were married on the 19th October 1899. I lived in his home for only two weeks, and understood a little of the difference between the husband's home and the wife's home. At the top there was my mother-in-law, then six or seven uncles, plus five older and younger aunts. I determined that in the future my daughters would be fully instructed before marriage to avoid the sufferings of a daughter-in-law. Oh my God! Although in my stupidity I had an aspiration, You in the end truly wrought for me.

After two weeks my husband took me to Shantou, where he was to work in the Maritime Customs office. After a year I had my oldest daughter, Guichen. After two more years, my second daughter Guizhen was born. Then my mother-in-law spoke. She said my husband's oldest brother's wife had six girls, and I must be like her, only able to have girls. The old lady also had the evil custom of esteeming boys and despising girls. But when I heard these words I completely disagreed, and said how was she able to know that I was a person not able to have boys, only girls? However, when I was pregnant again I really was a little fearful lest what the old lady said should be true.

It was strange, at this time when I could not do anything, when I had a grievance and no place or time for redress, that I should think of God Almighty and that I should rise up and beseech Him. In my stupidity I also remembered that story of Hannah. So I poured out my heart's desires before the face of God who hears prayers. In my heart I also believed He had answered my prayer and accepted my offering. When the time of birth came, I had a son. My husband, the first to see it was a son, immediately came to my ear and said, 'It's true, it is a son, thank God.' When I heard, I was happy, and thanked the Lord that He had heard my prayer and removed my shame. I was happy beyond expression.

Each time I was pregnant my mother came from Fuzhou to Shantou to serve me and look after me, lest others should be inadequate. But although she thus laboured with good will, I thought she was receiving the penalty for her own sins: if she had not caused me to be married in the first place, would I not be paying attention to her? I only now know how much I owed to my dear mother and feel the sorrow of a child when the parent is dead.

Several months after giving birth to my son, it happened that it was my father's sixtieth birthday. My mother wanted me, my husband and children to go home and honour him, and this is a duty children should perform, so we took a boat and returned to Fujian. The day after we got home, how could we know that my mother-in-law thoroughly disliked our first going to my mother's home and then to hers?

She said, 'Have you just arrived today?'

We replied, 'We arrived yesterday evening.'

She immediately said, 'Although the flood is great, it cannot sweep away a stone mortar.'[2] I immediately put the child I held into her hands. She could only force herself to receive him, and said to him, 'Where have you come from? Did you come by lot or are you an exchange?'

Oh! I thought she would be pleased to see the child, but

---

[2] A Chinese proverb.

as soon as I heard her speak like this my heart was cut with a knife. I was extremely hurt, and I did not know what to do for the best.

From this time my mother-in-law's home became my fiery furnace. Although I stayed in my mother's home, at times I thought, no matter how, my mother-in-law is my husband's mother and I am her daughter-in-law, so I ought to go and see her. So I bought and took a filial gift. As soon as she saw me she said coldly, 'You've come again!' This cool behaviour truly cut to my bones, but on the surface I could smile and say, 'Yes.' I really could not think of anything else suitable to say lest I add oil to the fire, and it would be all the more irreparable. So everybody was silent for a while, then I took my leave and returned to my mother's home. Although my mother and brothers had no objection to me staying a long time, my mother-in-law would not like it, but if I went to her home I could not endure her coolness and all the inconvenience. All we could do was to go back to Shantou. After this I had many children, altogether five boys and four girls. By the Lord's grace, they all grew up.

My husband's income at the Maritime Customs office was limited: thirty-five taels a month, which equals fifty-three dollars. It was necessary to send twenty-five dollars to my mother-in-law to support the home, leaving twenty-eight dollars. The rent was five dollars a month, leaving twenty-three dollars to live on. The children increased year by year. How could we live? But God is a merciful God, and opened the way for me. In Shantou the business of drawn-thread-work was very profitable. On the one hand I wrote to my father asking him to do the selling for me, and on the other hand I started to buy drawn-thread-work and all kinds of figured cloth and piece goods. God is worthy to be praised! Thus in the first year a lot of money was earned. Later, the more we did this, the more expert we became, and we sent goods to England, America, Singapore, Egypt, Shanghai and Hong Kong. Thus the bringing up of our children was not difficult.

Not long afterwards, my husband was transferred from Shantou Maritime Customs to Suzhou. At that time we really did not know what to do. Should we abandon the Maritime Customs profession and stay in trade in Shantou, or should we stop the trade and stay in Customs? Because the Customs position was permanent, and trade was dependent on fortune, my husband decided for the whole family to go to Suzhou. Fortunately, God's almighty hand was upon us in these dark days.

After a year a letter came from my mother-in-law wanting my husband to ask the Commissioner of Customs for leave of absence to return to Fujian, because the old and young at home needed somebody to look after them. My husband was a loyal son. When he saw the letter he immediately applied to the Commissioner. By the end of the month the concession was made. I rejoiced exceedingly at the thought of seeing my parents' family, but because of neglect of care after childbirth I was extremely weak, and had to let my husband and children return first to Fujian. I myself was cared for in hospital for several months, and then returned.

After returning home, I stayed in my mother's house for the greater part because it was comparatively convenient. In my heart I very much wanted to rent another house for my family, but my courage was small and I dared not speak. I could only keep silent and restrain my anger for the time being.

In 1911 it happened that the revolutionary army began, and I was patriotic towards the Nationalist Army and tried with the utmost effort to help. At that time shooting was fierce, regardless of life, and there were lectures everywhere. I first sacrificed adornments and gold bracelets to the country, making myself an example, and naturally many men and women followed suit. The Fujian government regarded my achievements as admirable. Mr Sun Daoren, the Governor of Fujian, especially asked the Beijing government to award me for my commendable work and patriotism. The result was that I was granted a second-class merit for loyal efforts rendered to the government. At this time I also sent letters to women in the region to form a Women's Patriotic Society. The wife of Governor Sun Daoren was President, the wife of Bian Shaosong was Vice President, and I myself was raised to General Secretary.

At this time I was much in contact with unbelievers, and naturally, before long, being a Christian with an empty profession, I dropped down to a place of unbelief, loving reputation, position, power, dress, etc. It can be said, in short, that I was a prodigal already come to the place of eating husks, but still self-exalted, contemptuous and truly foolish and pitiable! During this period I indulged myself in having fun, going to the cinema, and was always busy in social entertaining.

When Mr Sun Yat-sen came to Fujian, the government asked me to be a special lady receptionist. At that time Mr Sun brought two young gentlemen as well as young ladies, and also a private lady secretary, Miss Song, who was a classmate of mine in the Shanghai Chinese-Western Girls' School. After we met, naturally there was some special affection, so from beginning to end I accompanied them on their rounds and attended every feast of the organisation. After three or four busy days they returned to Shanghai.

Physically I could not bear any more, and had a serious illness, but I was still patriotic as if drunk or in a dream, mixing with friends. I went to worship no more, and long ago I had cast prayer behind me. Worse than this was that I went out of the way to discover faults in members of the congregation. When I happened to attend worship, if what the pastor said was good, I said he did not practise what he preached. If what he preached was not good, I said, 'This man who does not measure himself is not ashamed, he has no reason and is most stupid.' Oh my God, how hateful this is! But thank God, He is not only Abraham's and Isaac's God, he is also Jacob's God.

Chapter 2

In 1920, in the middle of the second month, a freelance lady missionary called Miss Yu Cidu came to Fuzhou to hold revival meetings. This lady I formerly knew slightly when I was in Shanghai. Moreover, I had special respect for her, because for the Lord's sake she had forsaken her medical vocation, fame and wealth, received no salary and was not hired by anyone, but solely preached, and trusted the Lord for supplies.

When I had seen her in Shanghai I unusually honoured her by passing on to her a ring my mother had given me. At first she was not willing to receive it and said, 'You are young; if the first time you see me you give me your ring, later when your mother knows you will be most sorry. You keep it.'

Hearing this, I surely knew she only loved the Lord, not things. I wept, definitely wanting her to receive it, and said, 'If my mother were to scold and beat me, I am willing.'

Then she smiled at me a little and said, 'Being so, I can only receive it. May God bless you.'

After this she went to Korea to preach. After an interval of twenty-two years, suddenly to hear the news that she was coming to Fuzhou to hold meetings was a prospect only those who have come through it can understand. Though I was pleased that she was coming, I also thought of my condition before God as truly unbearable to imagine – even the outward mask of a Christian had all gone. Her arrival gave me a huge jolt.[3] What could I do? If I said I was not pleased, she was also the one I most respected among Christians. Truly no pen and ink can describe this turmoil of happy and shameful thoughts.

The day before she arrived someone told me what time she was due, what time the meeting began, etc., so I decided to invite her to my home for the evening meal on the second day. Besides her I also invited one or two church members, and the remainder were my gambling friends. During the feast I spoke of her, and how she loved the Lord, etc. At the end I said, 'Tomorrow morning at eight o'clock, she will preach at the Heavenly Peace Hall – please all go.'

They all immediately said, 'And you?'

I answered, 'Of course I will go.'

So on the 15th of the second month, 1920, I woke up in the morning and straightaway prepared to go and listen to the word. On the first day she preached about how Adam lost life in the Garden of Eden. On the second day she followed up the first day's subject. I listened impatiently, and decided I would not go on the third day, for I had heard this subject since I was a child and knew it all. What was there to listen to? So on the third and fourth days I again played mah-jong with my gambling friends. They all said, 'We've wasted two days without playing mah-jong. The preaching

---

[3] Literally 'stab'.

is entirely unintelligible.' Although I did not say so, in my heart I knew they were wrong. Moreover, in playing that day they were all elated and happy. As for myself, however, I was like one about to die and sat there as one without a soul, with a bitter suffering in my heart I could not express. It was as though I would cry, and yet I did not know why, but really it was the Holy Spirit already working in my heart.

Altogether this condition went on for two days, and I could not go and play cards again. I could only announce, 'I am a Christian. I ought to go and hear the word. Miss Yu came here from a great distance to preach, and as I am so near the place, how can I decline to go? Not to go would be a breach of human propriety, not to say heavenly standards. No matter what, I am not coming to play, truly not coming!' From that day to this, twenty-three years by the grace of the Lord, I truly have not gambled again.

On the fifth day I awoke at four o'clock in the morning and could not sleep again. I could only get up and prepare to go again to the Heavenly Peace Hall to hear the word. As soon as I went in, Miss Yu immediately asked why she had not seen me the last two days.

I replied, 'I wasn't very well.'

She said, 'May God shine upon you and bless you so that you will be well very soon.'

Oh, how strong were these words coming from her mouth! They illuminated my heart and made me see that although I was not very well, how could I go and play cards but not be able to go and hear the word? Why shirk and lie? Alas! I, in darkness, had all my life boasted of being upright, and this was the first time I recognised myself as a liar. At this time I could not stop feeling nervous, and did not know what to do for the best. The time for the meeting had come, and I could only sit down. This day's subject was about the ways of nominal Christians, without reality, and she often pointed to me and said many piercing words, which truly made it uncomfortable to sit there. To get up and go would not be good, however, so I could only harden my face and listen.

At the end of the meeting she came again and asked me to come the next day. I thought, I am forty years old this year; from my parents down to my children, nobody has dared to sin against me like this, reproving me to my face – it would be good not to remain on the earth. That day, without cause, I came and received her anger. I had already determined that after that I would not come again, but now thus to be invited by her was troublesome: I could only nod my head.

When I got home I felt it was both exasperating and laughable. It was not that others had scolded me; it was I myself who had entered the door. What more could be said? I wondered how she knew about the affairs of my life. Surely somebody had told her. I thought further it must be her interpreter. I set my mind on having a dispute with her, but I had no proof. Such a matter could not be handled recklessly, for if it were not she, the consequences would be hard to deal with. Because of this I had to endure sickness, and could not sleep all night.

I had previously decided that on no account would I go the next day, but unconsciously within me there was an unspeakable strength urging me to go. So, strangely, I went again. That day she again followed up on the life of unreal Christians, as though she had seen my way of life with her own eyes. I sat there as though yesterday she had not scolded me enough: today I came again and allowed her to scold to her greater pleasure. I was most regretful and determined that no matter what, I would not come again. Thank God, several days' decisions not to go were all defeated – I went as before. Now I know this was Christ's victory and the devil's defeat.

On another day the preaching was about God's love and how the Lord Jesus on the cross Himself died instead of us and bore the punishment for our sin, so that we, because of His death, might not perish. She also said that the Lord on the cross had a body of flesh. What He endured was most painful and the shame most dreadful, but because He loved us He did not regard all this but willingly gave Himself and came to be the Saviour of mankind. I listened to this point and my hardened heart unconsciously was melted by this lovable Lord who gave His life for me. I wept, and wanted to offer Him all I had. I was even willing to be an evangelist to recompense Him.

After the meeting, when I got home, my husband saw me weeping unusually and said, 'When people go to worship they are all happy. You went and for several nights you can't sleep or eat. After this you needn't go any more.'

I said, 'You don't know the matter within. I know that I am a great sinner. God knows all my sin; now I know also because God has given me to see. Formerly, when you gave me housekeeping money, I left a little for gambling and did not use it all for the home. What a sin this was! Please forgive me.'

My husband then said, 'This is women's usual behaviour; it is nothing remarkable.'

I also told him of my unfaithfulness in serving him, and my deceit. I openly confessed all.

He said, 'Speaking so, how I too have sinned against you! Please also forgive me.'

Then we both wept. I thought that after this, husband and wife would surely love each other much better than before, but who could know it was certainly not so?

God also showed me I ought to confess my sin to my eldest son, but I was very unwilling. One day I took three dollars and bought a hymn book and New Testament for family worship. Just when I had chosen a hymn and was about to play and sing, the Spirit of the Lord was powerful within me and would not let me play. I must first confess my sin to my eldest son before He would let me sing and worship. I then said, 'O God, I am the mother: how can I confess to my son? After this, how could I pass the days in the home?'

God very clearly said, 'Without confession you cannot!' Then I could only submit to the Lord.

My husband and son saw I was going to play but did not. They only saw streaming tears and did not know why. But I turned and embraced my son and wholly confessed to him, saying, 'For the Lord's sake, I confess to you that the time when I beat you unjustly was a sin against you. Please forgive me.'

Everybody was surprised at me doing this, but my own son said, 'I truly hated you for beating me without cause that day.'

I said, 'Please forgive me.'

He did not answer, but that night the Lord gripped him. The next day he told me that he also was willing to go and hear the word and offer his heart and life to God for the ministry of preaching. As to how he was born again and offered himself to God, you all know from his own testimony. It is needless for me to recount it here.

Oh my God, although I have not forgotten my promise and offering to You before my eldest son was born, I am not concerned about how it is to become a reality. But You are God, and not only have You accepted my promise and offering, but You Yourself have perfected the accomplished fact. Just as the Scriptures say, 'For it is God who works in you both to will and to do of His good pleasure' (Philippians 2:13). Today he is already a servant of the Most High God. May glory and praise be unto God for ever. Amen!

After this God also required me to go and confess my sin to Miss Yu, namely that on the third and fourth days I went to play mah-jong but made the excuse that I was not well, which was a lie. I must go and face it clearly. I said, 'My God, how hard this is! Call it settled.' But God pressed me that I must go. Oh my friends, when man wants to commit a sin Satan makes it appear small and tells you it does not matter, you need not pay heed to speaking quite correctly, it is not reckoned as sin. From the beginning he swindled man like this. And when man is enlightened by God to know that sin ought to be faced, Satan uses a different method and enlarges sin so that man dare not confess. Oh my God! If it were not for dependence on Your grace and power, who could see this? Who is willing to confess sin and lose face? Truly through the love of the cross there is strength and enabling for man to obey.

I therefore responded to the Lord and duly went. The first time I went Miss Yu was not at home, and I returned.

The second time there was a guest with her. Then a little doubt arose within me as to whether God really wanted me to do this. Why on both these occasions had it been entirely inopportune? So I knelt down and prayed, 'Oh Lord, I have already been twice; why has it been quite inopportune?' Then God enlightened me and revealed the craftiness within me. I had gone in person, but my heart was not willing, so although I went it was no use. God is a God who searches men's secret feelings, so this time I confessed my sin before the Lord and asked for His forgiveness and strength. Truly I saw the hatefulness of sin and that it ought to be quickly faced and the opportunity not missed. Just before I went the third time, I first humbled myself before God and asked for His grace and strength, that I might do all well to His full satisfaction, without the least pretence. Certainly this merciful God treated me graciously.

When I went to Miss Yu's room and knocked at the door, she said, 'Come in.'

I then went in, and unexpectedly tears fell. I said to her, 'Miss Yu, I have sinned against you; I deceived you.'

She said, 'Since I came to Fuzhou you have treated me very well.'

I said, 'That day you asked me why I hadn't been for two days, I deceived you by saying I wasn't well, but I went to play cards. Now I ask you to forgive me.'

She said, 'Yes, this is sin. I forgive you, and my God also forgives you. Before you told me I already knew about you playing cards.' She then prayed with me and I unloaded my heavy burden and went home very happily.

One Wednesday evening after the prayer meeting, Pastor

Zhen Guantao came and asked me to be responsible for a class of pupils[4] the next Lord's Day, and I consented.

On Friday morning God also required me to go and confess to my third aunt. I hated her because she constantly ridiculed and criticised me and slandered me a great deal among my sons and daughters. I really was angry, with no redress for my grievance except to vent my anger on my own sons and daughters. Today my God required me to go and confess to her, and I was greatly disturbed. I knelt down and said, 'Oh God, it was she who first sinned against me, trumping up all kinds of bad language and slander, but You want me to go and confess to her. How can I?'

God said, 'I am holy, and you must be holy or I cannot use you nor wish you to teach in the Lord's Day school on Sunday. I can only put you aside.'

On Friday and Saturday I was unwilling to go and passed the days at home in a great battle. If I did not go, I was afraid God would be displeased and would not use me. If I went, I was afraid my aunt would shame me. My thoughts went back and forth, caught in a problem that was unspeakably bitter. On Sunday morning at four o'clock I asked God what to do, and within He very clearly said, 'Trust, go and confess, and I will tell you again.' I knew that confession could not be avoided. Because the love of the cross compelled me to obey God, I got up, combed my hair, washed my face and went.

My husband asked me, 'Where are you going?'

I answered, 'I am going to confess sin.'

---

4 Probably adults.

He promptly said, 'Don't be crazy. It's all right to confess sin at due times, but why this early?'

I could only smile at him, and went downstairs. My elderly servant, who had served me in the home for many years, also asked me, 'Madam, where are you going this early? You can't go without eating something.' Seeing I was firm about going and the rice in the pot was not yet cooked, she just took out a bowl of rice water and made me drink it before she would let me go. I had to accept her love, and drank it.

When I was halfway there I was truly afraid, and I hesitated.[5] Oh my Father, my God! But for Your great power to carry me through, I surely could have turned back. But God, whose grace is sufficient for me to use, gave me strength. I arrived at my mother-in-law's home and saw my aunt. She was upstairs doing her hair. Seeing me, she said in a tone of contempt, 'Is there something special that you have come so early?'

My heart pounded and I just said, 'I have come to ask your forgiveness. I have hated you and been angry with you, and it was sin. Please, for the Lord's sake, forgive me.' (It was she, with several fervent church members, who had invited Miss Yu to come at this time.)

When I stopped speaking, she said, 'I knew before that you were no good; it is fortunate that today God has enabled you to see it for yourself. Your sins are very many. It is not only a matter of sinning against me!'

How could I, who am passionate, regard this kind of behaviour lightly? Truly I can do all things through the Lord

---

[5] Literally, 'took three steps forward and two steps backward'.

who strengthens me. I very quietly said, 'I am going home now.' She nodded.

On the way I could not stop crying and feeling distressed, but in my heart I also had unspeakable peace and joy, because I knew my Lord was pleased and I had done what He wanted me to do. Here I saw a different outcome to the confession of sin. With my husband it led to him seeing a little of his own sin. With my son it brought him to know God's great power, to see his own sin, and to submit under the mighty hand of God and belong to Him. I was just the vessel. As for Miss Yu, it caused me to see light and love flowing from her. With my aunt, I am afraid to say what I saw; I might be wrong – may God Himself judge.

After I had confessed my sin I went home and had breakfast, then went to worship, conscious that I had the Lord's word and strength. Although I was not versed in the Scriptures, all I spoke was God's word. The listeners marvelled, and so did I. It was as though I had just graduated from God school. Everyone showed their pleasure and from then on I went to teach them every Lord's Day.

One day, conscious that my sins were so many, and knowing that my heavenly Father is merciful, I nonetheless wondered how He could be willing to forgive all. Consequently my position was uncomfortable, and I realised that this question must be solved. So I knelt down before the Lord and asked Him to direct me clearly. Our merciful God is gracious. As I was asking Him how I could hear His voice to explain this question, within me a voice said, 'My sheep hear My voice.' I thought I also heard, 'You are not the Lord's sheep, so you cannot hear His voice.' It was all because the preaching of the gospel at that time was not clear that there was this mistake. Even so, the truth can never be overthrown.

I saw there was a Bible on the table, and knew its contents were God's words. I had not read the Bible for many years: how could I know what He said? Ignorantly I scanned Genesis and Revelation and found nothing. In several books in the middle I found nothing. I could not think what to do, and wept and prayed before the Lord, saying, 'Oh God! If You are willing to forgive my sin and save me from being cast into hell and take me to heaven, I devote myself to preaching the word, for I am not willing to be an unreal Christian, not daring to accept the world yet not able to enter heaven.'

Oh, how hazardous is this fearful kind of prayer and approach! God is God. Who dares to contradict and set terms in His presence, asking Him to speak? I, who am worthy of death, can only say that God had mercy on my stupidity. Acts 17:30 says, 'The times of ignorance God overlooked, but now he commands all men that they should everywhere repent.'

At that time I took up the Bible and, following a very bad method, decided the answer to my question. First I closed the Bible, shut my eyes and said, 'Left-hand page, verse six.' On opening my eyes and turning the leaves of the Bible, I saw, 'Flee out of the midst of Babylon and save every man his life; be not cut off in her iniquity, for it is the time of the Lord's vengeance; he will render unto her a recompense' (Jeremiah 51:6). At that time, although I had not read the Bible for many years, I could still understand that it said my sin was as great as Babylon's and I must flee for my life. If we live in the midst of sin, we must perish with sin. God is a God who hates sin, yet He is a God who loves men. He also caused me to see the fear of sin and made me fear a sinful heart, and because of this all day long from morning to evening I was busy confessing sin and risked my life working. Although my heart had peace and joy, it was as though I only trusted in confession and works for salvation.

One day Satan came and said, 'It is not necessary for you to work, because you are always sinning, your temper is very bad and doesn't glorify God. You can't go to heaven.'

Then I thought, 'What can I do?' I could only kneel down and say, 'Lord, after all, can't I go to heaven?'

Within me a voice very clearly asked, 'The everlasting life which you received, whose life is it?'

I answered, 'Lord, it is Your life.'

Within He asked again, 'From whom did My life come?'

I answered again, 'From the life of God the Father.'

He said again, 'Because you have My life and the life of the Father within you, you won't be cast into hell, but will go to heaven. Even if you went to hell's door, the devil would see that the Father and I are within you, and would certainly say, "You have come to the wrong place, this is not your place – be gone quickly."'

From this I had a complete assurance that I would go to heaven and not be cast into hell. Afterwards a much clearer voice within said, 'If you were cast into hell, would not God and I be cast in with you?' Then I understood more clearly that it is because I have God's life within me that I can go to heaven and not be cast into hell. It does not in the least depend on our actions, but entirely on God's grace, as the Bible tells us (in Ephesians 2:8–9 and Romans 11:5–6). Oh! The almighty, all-wise God knows that there is nothing we can do to obtain salvation, and He is gracious to man and only requires us to be willing to come and receive saving grace and escape perdition and freely have eternal life. So I was full of joy, and I praise and worship our God for ever. Amen.

Chapter 3

One day I said to the Lord, 'Ought I to leave home and go and study theology?' It so happened that Miss Pamiter, a theological professor, was leading meetings in Fuzhou, so I asked her opinion on my question. Thanks be to the Eternal God that He can lead a mistaken one to go the right way. God, through her, said to me, 'You need not go and study theology. You ought to serve God at home.' I had been full of enthusiasm, hoping she would say, 'You should go and study theology.' Yet when I heard her words, I was truly able to cast off my rash and foolish zeal. Today as I write, I still value what she saw before the Lord.

Again another day I said to the Lord, 'Oh God! When I previously promised You that I would devote myself to evangelism, was it really from myself, or did man come and ask me to go? I do not know, please show me.'

Just as I finished praying, somebody knocked on the door downstairs and said to my servant, 'Does your mistress believe Christianity is true?'

My servant replied, 'Certainly it is true.'

This person then said, 'Is she earnest in it?'[6]

My servant said, 'I don't know about that.'

I then went downstairs and asked the visitor everything. She said to me, 'There is a Mr Lin Changshou who has come from Nanyang, and there are demons where he lives. A little girl has already been seized, and now a boy is sick, so they want to ask someone who genuinely believes in Jesus and has implicit faith to go to their home to pray for them and cast out the demon. Do you think you can go?'

As she said this I was silent, then after a moment I said, 'If you want somebody who truly believes in Jesus, I honestly tell you I do. Although you have seen me before, at that time I was only a nominal Christian. Now it is true that I have the life of the Lord Jesus within me, but as to being earnest or mature, I am not.'

At once she said, 'If you are true, that is enough, because we don't know who is an earnest one. Please come with me, because the child will soon die. His mother is holding him in her arms waiting for you.'

'Oh my God,' I thought, 'what does this child understand, who has only been born again a few months?'

Just as I was in this dilemma, within me a voice said, 'This is God's answer to my prayer, and the work He wants me to do.' I also remembered it was like our brother Peter praying on the roof-top, and downstairs the messengers from Cornelius were looking for him.

I then wonderingly went with her, with inexpressible joy within. The people who asked me and desired a true and deep believer in the Lord thanked God. Although I was not

---

[6] Literally, 'deep in it'.

mature, nevertheless I truly had the Lord Jesus; if not, how this whole family would have lost hope! Supposing I not only had not attained maturity but also had no genuine faith – how pitiable that would have been!

On arriving at that home I saw that Mr and Mrs Lin Changshou's circumstances were as though they were in a great drought, hoping for rain. I then knelt down and prayed and asked the Lord to teach me what to do. Then I got up and began to preach the gospel, proving that the Lord Jesus is God's Son and the Saviour of men. I knelt down again and prayed, and this whole family believed and accepted the Lord Jesus as their Saviour, and the child was healed. Oh dear Lord Jesus Christ, You are God's Son and the Saviour of men, and the physician of the sick. Truly You should be thanked, praised and worshipped unto eternity. Amen.

After this, every Tuesday at 2 p.m. there was a Bible study meeting in my home. Mr Huang Shangte and Pastor Xi Zezhao were responsible for it. We studied the prophecies and the Lord's coming again. Also, both within and without the city there were big revival meetings. They had the preaching responsibility and I invited people and played the music, and we were busy for several months.

One day a Methodist church member asked me to speak at a Sunday evening prayer meeting. At the time when Pastor Zhen Guantao asked me, my heart trembled. I was very fearful because the Methodist Heavenly Peace Hall is a big hall, and there were not a few important people there. I knew I was unworthy to stand on the platform and immediately answered, 'I can't do this.'

As soon as the words were out of my mouth a voice

within me said, 'Why did you not ask Me, and why did you say "I can't"?'

Being so, I did not know what it was best to say. But this pastor repeatedly asked me to respond, so I could only say, 'Let me pray and see, and we will speak about it again.'

He further said, 'This is the Lord's service; it is always good. I need an answer today, as I have the responsibility of inviting a speaker for Sunday evening.'

Then the Lord gave me grace to know it was His will for me to testify at this hall on Sunday evening, so I replied, 'All right.'

All the way home my heart was very happy to have the opportunity to witness for the Lord, but I was afraid I would be unable. The whole night was peaceful, but Satan raised his head and began to work. The next day somebody said to me, 'There is an American missionary who is very angry that you interpreted for several days for Miss Yu Cidu, saying how could a sinner like you interpret!' As soon as I heard this report, I immediately had one thought: if I should not interpret, how much more should I not preach at the Heavenly Peace Hall.

I went upstairs to write to the pastor, saying that I would not speak. But when I took up the pen I could not write. I was so extremely distressed that I could only kneel down and pray, and I had an indescribable urge within which did not allow me to shirk witnessing for the Lord. I then said, 'I will go.' Peace and joy then filled my heart.

After this I daily sought a subject, not knowing which verse of Scripture I ought to use. I was also not well versed in the Scriptures. I looked and prayed, and prayed and looked, and within was led to John 3:16 as the subject, but, being corrupt, I regarded it as too familiar. But praying back and forth, the Lord only gave me this verse. The Lord should be praised. He cannot fail, for He is God.

On that Lord's Day morning I went as usual to worship and heard Pastor Wang Ganhe preach, and he preached very well. As I listened I thought, 'What about this evening?' The more I thought, the more I wanted to trust God, but I could not – countless prayers did not avail. At six o'clock in the evening I began to weep as though I were being dragged out to death. Nevertheless, I could not but go.

I was the first one to arrive at the hall. There was nobody around, so I knelt alone and prayed earnestly, asking the Lord to give grace that what I said would glorify His name. Afterwards a lot of people gradually came, among them many who came specially to hear me; that evening there were particularly many. When I went up to the platform there immediately came upon me an inexpressible power and fullness of grace, and new light and life. I spoke that which I had not thought of, and the more I spoke the more I had. I spoke for over an hour. After prayers, several foreign sisters and Chinese pastors came and grasped my hand, saying, 'Today it was not you speaking, it was God.' Oh, how true and comforting were these words! An American teacher of theology, Miss Meace, shook hands and asked me to go to Fuqing county to hold revival meetings in a women's theological college, where she held responsibility. I nodded, and dared not refuse.

There was one truly remarkable thing – namely, that when Miss Yu Cidu left Fuzhou, she gave me the straw bag which she herself daily used to carry her Bible when she travelled evangelising. She said, 'You will carry on my work, so I give you my Bible bag.' After a year, when she came to Fuzhou again, she also gave me a very good leather Bible bag which she had brought from England, and said, 'This bag will last you a lifetime.' True, although I was already 43 years old, a bag like this was certainly useful.

One day I received an invitation from Miss Xi of the YWCA to stay at her place for sixteen days to speak daily to the faculty and members of the association. After the meetings Miss Xi wanted me to rest for a few days. Physically I really needed to rest after this heavy work, but because I dare not be lord of my own life, I placed the matter before the Lord. While I was praying, the Lord very clearly required me to go home and gave me to see that at home something unthought-of would arise. I therefore declined Miss Xi's kind invitation and immediately returned home, where I found everybody, old and young, in peace. Although it was so, I knew God could not make a mistake.

That evening my husband walked with me outside the front door. Suddenly my spirit was moved and I knew there would be a fire that night, and I told my husband. He did not say a word, and we went to bed. At 3 a.m. indeed a big fire soared to the sky and people's voices filled our ears. We awoke from a dream and prayed to the Lord and He gave me to see that our house would have perfect safety, so I was at peace. Although there were quite a few children in the house, I was not in the least agitated. When the fire had reached as far as next door but two to my house, suddenly the wind turned its direction strongly and the fire burnt more than ten other people's houses. In this matter God also gave me to see that my believing in and relying on Him had saved the great fuss in which the whole family might have been involved. This is God's great grace, and I worship Him.

A week later my husband and I were walking to and fro in the same way outside the front door. At this time I was moved again in my spirit and knew that there would be another fire that night, and I told my husband this. I was surprised when he frowned at me and said, 'Don't be funny.' I did not answer, and we parted unhappily.

That night at four o'clock the sound of calling outside was much louder than the previous time, and the fire was helped by much rain and strong wind. This time my husband said to me, 'As you see it, will our house be involved this time?' I then put his question to the Lord. The Lord gave me to see that it could be burnt, so I told my husband and household, and we began to put our clothes and things in cases, preparing to move elsewhere.

Again a strong voice within me said, 'Although the situation is like this, why don't you pray?' This brought to mind our forefather Abraham praying for Sodom and Gomorrah. He began praying for fifty righteous people, moving down to ten, and the Lord was willing to grant his request. But there were not even ten righteous people, and Abraham was not willing to move downwards again, and the two cities consequently met with calamity and destruction. But truly God is a God unwilling for any to perish, so He sent two angels to save a righteous man, Lot, who was failing and degenerating.

Thinking of this, I stopped collecting things and knelt down and prayed, 'Oh God, in this district of Fuzhou my family is the only one which believes in You; if my house is

burnt together with those of unbelievers, what is the difference between us and them? Moreover, won't they be able
to ridicule us, saying, "Where is your God?" How could I
answer them?'

I truly thank and praise Almighty God that all power is in
His hands. He gave me this prayer, and immediately said to
me, 'Though a thousand shall fall at thy side, and ten thousand at thy right hand, this calamity will not come near
you' (Psalm 91:7). Oh, how happy I was to get God's word!
Right away I told my husband and family that it was not
necessary to collect things any more, for God had spoken to
me. But not one of them was willing to believe me now. I
alone sat peacefully in a chair, ceasing from all work, just as
if there were no fire.

My husband, seeing that the fire was fierce and the wind
and rain increased, could not restrain great anger, and he
opened his mouth and scolded me, saying, 'Don't be crazy;
one time you say the house will burn, and another time you
say it won't. It is all rubbish you are uttering, while with all
these children you don't even help me to collect things
quickly.'

My resolve weakened by his scolding, I got up and turned
clothes and things from drawers into a case. Just then, suddenly, a hand patted my left shoulder and a voice said, 'Oh
you of little faith, why didn't you believe what I said?' I
immediately knelt down and wept bitterly before the face of
my Lord who loved me, and asked Him to forgive my sin.
I, of course, no longer paid any attention to the clothes. My
husband thought my crying was due to his rebuking and so
he grumbled a great deal more. What he actually said I was
not minded to listen to carefully, as my weeping was

certainly because I had not listened to what the Lord said and had sinned against Him – how could it have been because of my husband's scolding? But he only saw me crying without understanding the real cause, and I did not attempt any explanation.

After a while the Fire Brigade arrived by boat at my front door. Because Fuzhou's several-hundred-year-old bridge had been suddenly blocked, they could only come up by boat. My front door was near the river bank, so the Fire Brigade used the doorway of my home as the issuing point of their operations. When the fire reached as far as three houses away from my home, the wind suddenly changed again and went elsewhere. Helped by the force of the water from the Fire Brigade, my house was preserved intact. At that time I did all I could to look after the needs of the firemen, and I also gave them a little reward. Everybody dispersed quite happily, and oh, how much happier I was! The God whom I serve, how sincere He is! I must worship before Him who has treated this chief of sinners so graciously.

Chapter 4

One day I received an invitation from the Methodist church in Mingqing county to go there and attend their seventieth anniversary meeting. They asked me to witness for the Lord in the girls' school there. Although I was not versed in the Scriptures, God gave me words as though I had just come out of theological school, and I was filled with the Holy Spirit's power, causing the whole school to weep bitterly, confess sin and repent.

One of the lady teachers of the theological school, hearing about this, was most displeased and acknowledged that this class of girls had been influenced by me. She said that if I went to speak at her women's theological school she would certainly oppose me. A few days later, however, Miss Jones, the American principal of that women's theological college, invited me to go and preach. I was fearful and dared not go. But that night the Lord said to me, 'Don't be afraid; you just go. I will go with you.'

Thanks be to God, after the message on the first day, the first one to repent and weep and confess sin to her fellow workers was the teacher who opposed me. I never would have thought that she could repent so quickly. Truly it was God Himself working.

When the sixteen days' ministry were ended, I thought to return home. Pastor Xi Zezhao and his wife had been invited and gone with me to Mingqing. I do not know how, but they heard a rumour that I would linger for a few days before returning home, so they left first. By the time I started to leave, there was only one vacant sedan chair. Of the chair-bearers, one was able-bodied; the other was an elderly man of about sixty, and according to what he said, the previous night he had seen an evening play and had not slept all night, so how could he have the strength to carry this stout lady, weighing more than 190 pounds? So as he carried he complained that I was too fat and too stout, and he said a lot that was unpleasant and rude. Then the Lord's grace truly filled my heart, so that not only was I not angry, but having the opportunity to suffer for my Lord, my spirit was incomparably happy. The more he cursed, the more I laughed, and the more I laughed, the more dangerously angry he became.

Within 50 *li*[7] of the wharf they set me down and would carry me no further. Then I could only get out of the chair and walk – but I wore high-heeled shoes, above me there was slight rain, and below a small path about one foot wide full of earthenware stones. Altogether it was a difficult walk, inch by inch. At first I used an umbrella handle as a staff, but before long the handle broke, and I could only ask the younger chair-bearer to take my hand and walk with me, because I had already fallen eight times. My disordered body and clothes were all stained with filthy mud and my hair was even more unbearably dishevelled. I was not fit to

---

7 A Chinese unit of distance; one *li* is about 0.4 mile.

meet anybody. Nonetheless, despite this, my face and heart were filled with peace and joy. Each time I fell I laughed heartily, making the two chair-bearers astonished. They urged me not to laugh, lest it should cause further falls, but I did not mind in the least and just continued to laugh. Now I know it was the Holy Spirit's outpouring.

After this Satan said to me, 'If you serve Jesus of Nazareth you will be unwell your whole life, and it will be very bitter. You can see that these pastors who believe in Jesus are also very bad; they cast you on one side. When you don't serve Jesus, how honourable you will be; when you travel you will have three men to carry your chair, and people will follow you – why suffer the hardship of travel like this?' Besides this, Satan also said a lot of unpleasant and laughable things, but I dismissed them all and took no notice.

When I reached the wharf I found that the pastor and his wife had already gone on ahead by boat, having waited for me in vain for two or three hours and decided I had surely lingered at Mingqing. Then I was truly in a strange place with strange people, and I did not know the way I should go. I could only shed tears and cry to the Lord, 'Oh Lord, please open the way for me.'

When I had prayed, I saw a man carrying a foreign lamp coming towards me. He was Mr Le Fuhua, son of aged Pastor Le Yingkuan. He saw that I was travelling alone at night and my clothes were untidy, and at once with unusual politeness asked me whether I had lost a companion along the road, and whether I needed his help. I hastened to tell him all the facts of the situation. He then most politely led the way to Dr Xi's residence in preparation for me to stay there overnight.

Who would have thought it, but as soon as Dr Xi saw us he looked quite unhappy for a few moments, and said his wife had gone to her mother's home and there was no woman to receive me, he feared it was not very convenient, etc., etc. But after waiting a while, probably his conscience could not rest, and he said that he would go to a friend for the night and leave me alone in his house. After I heard this a big load dropped from my heart. The two men prepared peanuts, salted egg and rice porridge. I also washed my clothes well and they dried them by the fire for me.

At about ten o'clock they took me to Mrs Xi's room. After prayer, I went to bed. I fully hoped to drop my head and sleep comfortably, but – who would have thought it? – Mrs Xi had gone to her mother's home more than a month earlier, added to which during that time there had been many successive rainy days, so between the coverlets there was an indescribable odour. How could I, who usually had an obsession for cleanliness, sleep? Because of this I turned back and forth, covered my nose with my hand, and was moved with great vexation. I did not know what to do for the best. Just then, suddenly, an honourable and lovable small voice said, 'I slept in an ox manger; is this bed not better than an ox manger?'

After hearing this I was greatly moved in my spirit, and I knew my sin. Then I immediately got up and knelt down and asked the Lord to forgive my sin, and I also asked Him to give me a will to suffer, so that I could suffer for Him. After prayers, I got into bed and lay down. I also asked the Lord to let me, like John, lean on His bosom.

Indeed, I had an agreeable night's sleep. When I awoke it was past five o'clock, and my spirit and body were happy and well. When I had washed and eaten breakfast, Mr Le said that he would go with me to Fuzhou. I praised God that He did not make me bear a burden that I could not carry, and I was profoundly grateful to Mr Le – he truly is not ashamed to be a pastor's son.

After I got home, because I had walked too much my body was very painful and I was constantly groaning. When my husband heard this he was very angry and abused me, saying such things as, 'You loafer, who told you to go? You come home ill and excel in annoying others. True nuisance!' This was the first time he was impolite to me in this way. Oh my God, it is truly strange that before I was saved, every time I came home from playing cards I always got into a great temper if he had not sent servants to prepare things properly. Today I go out on the Lord's work and he reviles me like this. Truly one cannot understand it. But we must suffer persecution, so I could only restrain my anger and say nothing; even in moaning I dare not let it all out. This was the first time I began a life of restraining my anger and saying nothing to my husband.

After three weeks like this had passed, the principal of Tuh Ing girls' school, seeing that I was weak in body and the children in my home were many, invited me to stay in her home for two weeks, and never fell short in the smallest details of caring for me. I therefore gradually became vigorous once again.

Not long after I got home, I was asked again by Miss Pamiter to go to Fuqing to preach the gospel. At that time foreigners for the most part did not highly esteem Chinese people, and she invited me to stay with and eat with the pupils. The food was dried sweet potato and a big bowl of greens. I can honestly say that I have never treated the servants in my own home so stingily. But I did not say a word, and was prepared to accept the arrangement. But right away the Lord cared for me, knowing that I could not eat the food. Just as I had finished praying, I saw brother Li Guichong's mother and Dr Huang standing beside me, and they took me by the hand and would not let me eat what the foreigners had prepared for me, but pressed me to go and stay with them. Not only did I sleep in their own bed, but the food was specially prepared for me and was abundantly ample. Thus I passed over a month, and when the ministry was over I returned home. This time I was not only not sick, I had gained twelve pounds. I truly thank and praise our God.

After some days I was asked to go again to Fuqing to minister on the twentieth day of the twelfth month, which was exactly the date of my second daughter's wedding. I spread this matter before the Lord and He very clearly gave me to know in my spirit that I ought to go forth and serve Him. But I was worried about how to manage the affairs of my daughter's wedding. Then the Lord also said to me, 'Did you not tell Me you loved Me more than everything else?'

I answered, 'Oh, Lord, yes.'

At that same time I also knew in my heart that this was an opportunity to prove that I did indeed love the Lord more than everything else. So I immediately gathered my luggage together, reckoning to go to Fuqing to work. Seeing this behaviour, my husband's anger rose to the skies; my second daughter, Guizhen, wept very much. Man is not wood and stone, and under these circumstances I could only think of a plan to go and see my husband's third younger sister and invite her to help with everything at my daughter's wedding. But who would have thought it? As soon as she heard this, she was not only unwilling to help, but gave a big grunt, saying, 'Guizhen has a mother. Why is it necessary for an aunt to help? I advise you not to be crazy. . .'

'Oh my God,' I said in my heart, 'no matter what, I want to love You more than anything else.' So I went on gathering my baggage, and my family regarded me as a great sinner. Then I again asked the Lord to glorify His own name, that in this matter I certainly might love Him and do His will obediently.

Before long a messenger came from the home of my son-in-law, Lin Puqi, to say that he was sick and the date for the wedding was changed to the 20th of the first month of the following year. When I knew this I was full of joy and thanked my heavenly Father, and the whole family was happy and let me go out in ministry. The ministry ended on the first day of the first month, and I returned home just in time to arrange my daughter's wedding fittingly. In this matter I saw that we only need to follow the Lord obediently and love Him, and our God Himself is able to order well for us.

After this I was asked again, for the third time, to go to Fuqing to minister. After the meetings I decided to return home, but it was pouring with incessant rain. Everybody pressed me to wait until the weather was fine, but before the Lord the only indication I had was to return home that day because there was a difficulty at home, so I asked the Lord to stop the rain. The Lord gave me to know in my spirit that the rain would stop, so I changed my prayer to praise.

At the time I started out it was still raining, but as the chair was borne out of the gate the sun suddenly came out and the umbrella which they made me take for the rain became a parasol. Writing now, I truly want to sing, 'Glorious grace, marvellous grace; from now and henceforth I will trust the Lord's grace.'

One day Miss Corlintone, an English lady, invited me to Gutian for ministry. The Lord wanted me to go, so I assented. When I arrived at Gutian she very gladly received me as a guest in her home. But there was a difficulty: she said that Bishop Hind of the church mission she belonged to had told her not to allow me to speak on baptism by immersion and leaving a denomination. As for the rest – doctrines of salvation and victory – I could suit myself and freely preach.

I immediately closed my eyes and inwardly asked the Lord until I had received guidance, then I asked her, 'Who do you say I am?'

She said, 'You are a handmaid of the Lord.'

I said, 'You are right. Since it is so, I cannot be lord of what I preach or don't preach – only Jesus is Lord. If the bishop wishes to restrict my subjects, I had better go home and not hold the meetings, for I truly haven't the courage to decide what I preach or don't preach.'

'Mrs Ni,' she said, 'you can regard the Lord as Lord: who am I to dare to oppose the Lord's maidservant? You just go and proclaim God's word far and wide. If the bishop knows and scolds me, or degrades me from office, I would be willing and happy.'

Because of this, we then began to work together as of one heart and mind. I also went to a good number of all the neighbouring country villages. Many places received God's blessing and truly those who repented and came to the Lord were not a few.

It was New Year time by the old calendar when I returned to Fuzhou from Gutian. Miss Corlintone especially instructed a servant to escort me back. To begin with I travelled by sedan chair. When I was going to board the boat, the servant who escorted me bowed deeply to me and said, 'Because I am a servant, my salary is trifling and does not meet expenditure, so I have opened a small shop besides as a means of assisting. At the close of this year I must go to the shop to settle accounts, so I cannot escort you back to Fuzhou. But if I do not escort you back and Miss Corlintone finds out, she will certainly dispense with me and that will be much worse. So bearing all this in mind, I implore you to go back by yourself, and also not to tell Miss Corlintone. If you are able to agree, I will be deeply grateful for your kindness.'

While he spoke he appeared most pitiable. This made me immediately ask God to show me what to do, because ordinarily I would have depended on him very much during the journey. Then God said to me, 'My child, the Lord will provide.' At once I responded to his request. He then went back rejoicing greatly, walking and glancing back, showing how very much he was obliged to me. As for me, I just had to rest in the Lord.

The first night on the boat was without incident. On the second day, as soon as it was light, I prayed, saying, 'Oh my Father God, You said You would provide. Now the time has come, please lead me.' I thus humbly mentioned it before the Lord and was conscious of abundant peace within.

After breakfast I opened the door of my room and went out, and I saw a man standing beside the door as if he were waiting for me. I could not help asking who he was and what he was doing standing there. He said, 'Last night at midnight I couldn't sleep; it was as though a man said to me that you needed someone to carry your luggage, and I was to come and wait at your door. So I have waited quietly for you for half an hour.'

I then said to him, 'It is the God whom I serve who told you to come and carry for me.'

He said, 'Since it is so, when the boat comes to the wharf, please sit quietly on the boat and when everybody has gone I will carry your luggage and take you across the pontoon.'

I nodded in assent. Afterwards he certainly carried out everything very well, even to paying out the charge of several coppers for me when we crossed the bridge. He also hired a small boat for me and accompanied me home. While we were on that boat he said to me, 'Everybody on the boat had their own luggage and couldn't carry for you, and although the remaining gentlemen themselves had no luggage, they couldn't carry either. Since I was the only coolie and had no luggage, I could be of service to you. This God of yours really is very knowing.' So I also preached the gospel to him.

When we arrived at Fuzhou he not only carried my luggage to the wharf and to my home, he even volunteered to carry it upstairs into my room. I gave him money, but he would not receive it; my third son brought a bowl of vermicelli and invited him to eat, but he declined it firmly. He said he had money, for his elder brother had sent back a hundred dollars from Nanyang and this journey had been made in order to go to the bank and withdraw the money, so he was empty handed and well able to carry luggage for me. Then he ran off chuckling. I truly thank and praise our faithful God with a full heart. I will ever regard His faithfulness to provide.

After this I was also invited to go to Nanping. Because we arrived late, the boat we had engaged was already taken by others. When we came to the wharf and saw this, we could not disguise our vexation. All we could do, however, was to hire another boat – both small and bad – because the date of the meetings was already fixed and we were therefore compelled to fulfil the commitment.

Unexpectedly, when the boat had not gone far, it was suddenly announced that there was a hole in the bottom and water was incessantly leaking into the boat. Then everybody worked: some devoted themselves entirely to bailing water, and some prepared bamboo shavings to stop up the hole. A lot of time, human strength and resources were expended before we could proceed. By that time everybody was out of sorts and could not help murmuring against heaven and blaming other people.

When we arrived at Nanping we learned that the boat we had first booked and which other people had taken had met with robbers and been plundered. Here we realised that it was well our own boat was small and bad, because the robbers took no notice of it. More wonderful was the fact that the hole in the bottom of the boat caused delay, so we did not even meet the robbers. 'All things work together for good to them that love God.' Beautiful words of God! I adore Him for ever.

After this I also went to Changlo to minister. As soon as Mrs Li, the evangelist there, saw me she said, 'Although you preach the gospel everywhere and the results are all very good, it won't work here. There is a saying criticising Changlo: "The fairies find it difficult to get people from Changlo."'

I recognised this was God's matter, and I was not concerned. For the first three days I just preached the Lord's good news. Very early on the fourth day, as soon as I awakened, I asked the Lord, 'Not only are people's hearts not moved in the least, but there is a cold atmosphere which is really unbearable. What can I do?'

The Lord said to me that it was all my fault. I was startled and said to the Lord, 'Do I not faithfully preach Your word? Why do You say it is all my fault?'

Our loving Lord then showed me, saying, 'Is there anything too hard for Me – Jehovah? I am God who changes nothing into something. Why didn't you ask Me?'

I immediately got up, combed my hair and washed, fasted and prayed, confessed my sin before God, and asked the Lord to change people's hearts. This was the first time I had fasted. Our compassionate and merciful God: He truly is a God who answers prayer.

That day, from eight o'clock in the morning when the meeting commenced, right up to the end, God's Spirit greatly filled me. At about half past one in the afternoon, it was really moving to see the condition of those who repented, confessed and wept bitterly. Only one person, Mrs Li, was obstinate and unmoved. It was very pitiable that God allowed her to see other people receiving grace like this, but she herself received nothing. The Bible is quite right in saying that everything is in the hands of our merciful God. Heaven and earth can change, but the word of the Lord can never change.

One day a sister invited me to her husband's birthday feast. At first I was unwilling to go, but within the Spirit of the Lord urged me to go. So, according to my inward leading, I went. On arrival there I saw a Mr Chen, who had come back from South-east Asia, and I began to ask him about the question of salvation. We spoke a few sentences, then immediately took our seats for the meal. No one guessed that God's Spirit was already moving in his heart. He did not sleep soundly the whole night, and very early the next day came to see me. I had already heard a rumour that this man was lacking in morality, so I was unwilling to meet him, but the Lord said to me, 'I preached to the woman of Samaria; are you more holy and honourable than I am? Go! Preach the word of life to him.' So I dared not make excuses and went downstairs to see him. That day he was saved by grace.

This man saw that many people had believed in the Lord for years, but did not yet know the way of salvation and thus led a confused life as if drunk or in a dream and were really to be pitied. He therefore decided to invite me to go to South-east Asia to preach the gospel. I dared not promise immediately, but sought the Lord's will. Three weeks later, the word the Lord gave me was Luke 4:43, 'But Jesus said to them, "I must also preach the gospel of the kingdom of God in other cities, for it was for this that I was sent."'

Since it was clear that I must go, I then asked God to give me a companion. Then I sent a telegram to Shanghai to ask my eldest son, Watchman, if he would go with me to

South-east Asia. Who would have thought it, but the word he received before the Lord was the same as I had been given, Luke 4:43! I did not know this until he spoke of it in testimony in South-east Asia. Then I could not help praising the Lord, saying, 'God's work is one thread.'

Chapter 5

On our arrival in South-east Asia we immediately began to work, but the pastor was not happy. He said, 'A month ago a pair of Americans, husband and wife, came here to hold revival meetings. All of us pastors put in much effort inviting church members to come and hear the word. The first day there were over three hundred people; the second there were over sixty; the third day there were only twelve people. Also now it is just the time for sapping the rubber trees and people haven't time to hear the word – they can only come on Sundays.' We did not mind what he said, but only knew within that the Lord's leading was absolutely correct.

On the second day, just before the time of the meeting, a few of us went to the church and saw the door was tightly closed. The key was at the pastor's place, so we had to go to his house to find him. We were astonished to find that he was still at home calculating how much rubber the workmen had brought in, and did not know that it was time for the meeting. Everyone there saw that we showed no embarrassment or displeasure – we just took up the key and went. As soon as we opened the church and went in, we saw countless white ants (because the building was made of *ya ta* grass). We borrowed a broom from somebody and swept the floor, and an Indian brother went out on the street to draw people in to hear the word. This was all because the pastor did not participate, so we just had to put forth the utmost effort ourselves.

At first only a few tens of people came, but, because the Lord worked greatly, by three o'clock in the afternoon when there was another meeting there were over one hundred people. The next day, we changed the meeting to begin at ten o'clock, because it was comparatively more convenient. Those who came increased to over three hundred. Each day there were meetings and each time not only were the seats full, but the space outside the hall was filled with people standing. Fearing they would not get a seat, some people came an hour early to the hall and waited quietly. Some even brought their noontime meal with them from home and ate it in the hall. Those who repented, confessed, wept in distress and were saved truly increased with the days – thanksgiving and praise be to the Lord.

Under these circumstances, the pastor came to us and said that doing things like these dramatic performances was not quite right. He was afraid that if his church members came to meetings like this every day they would be too tired, and he asked us to close the meetings. I then answered him, 'If they are too tired, they will decide for themselves not to come. Please do not worry.' Thus we preached the gospel for about sixteen days. Afterwards we had Bible studies to help them see something of the way and the truth.

After this, numerous telegrams came from every area in

South-east Asia inviting us to go and minister. By the grace of the Lord, where we ought to go we went, and where we ought not to go, or where it was not clear, we did not go. We worked in South-east Asia for about six months, then returned to China. Passing through Shanghai, we were asked by Dr Shi Meiyu of the Bethel Hospital to minister for ten days. The Chinese-Western Girls' School also asked me to minister for a week. The school superintendent, Miss Ma Xiuying, saw with her own eyes the difference between me now and when I studied there. She was very, very pleased, and praised God.

At this time I could not preach entirely in Mandarin. I preached in Fuzhou dialect and sister Xi Qinde interpreted for me. When the ministry was ended I came to Fuzhou and was ill for a long time. One day God led me to ask a neighbour from Tianjin to come and teach me, my youngest daughter and two young sons to read the Psalms in Mandarin. After a few months the Mandarin teacher said that out of the four pupils, he reckoned the old lady of over fifty was the best. Now I can freely use Mandarin in prayer, preaching, etc. Is not this the grace of God? May glory be to Him for ever. Amen.

Several months later, Heavenly Peace Hall elected the president and officials for the Sunday evening Necessity of Virtue Society. Watchman and I were both there. Truly unexpectedly, the papers nominating me numbered eighty-eight. The old president then said that although I had the most votes, it was not more than half and we should vote again. But when the second vote was taken, the highest number, which this time was also more than half, again fell on me. So I was duly elected president. Not only did I not want this, but my whole body trembled and I wanted to stand up to decline. Nobody noticed me, however. They were all there full of spirits and elated, rejoicing that I had been elected president of the Necessity of Virtue Society. How could I, pitiable, just saved and unworthy, take this important position? But since the Lord sanctioned it, He also took the responsibility for me, and together the people also helped. After this I was recommended as leader of the Prayer Group and also of the Moral Culture Group of the YWCA. Before long, Mrs Gao Ji revealed a heart for the Chinese Women's Fellowship, and everybody recommended her as president of the society and me as vice-president.

At that time I was as though drunk or in a dream concerning the sin in me, thinking, 'Now I have had a great crisis, and what I do is entirely spiritual work.' Actually it was not. Now, when I think of what I did then, I can see that not only was it without profit, it was injurious. Writing at this time, I can only bow my head and ask the Lord to forgive my ignorance, for that is born of the flesh, but that which is born of the Spirit is Spirit.

One day I went to my mother school and saw Mrs Xi Tang. She told me that Miss He Shouen[8] had twice wanted to see me but hadn't. The first time I truly had responded to Miss Mei's invitation to go to Mingqing for meetings; the second time I received Miss Pan's invitation, so we did not meet on either occasion. She also said she had something she wanted to tell me. I really didn't know of anything special, but when I got home I told Watchman.

Just before Easter Watchman came and said to me,

---

[8] The English missionary Margaret Barber (see photo p. 83).

'Mother, from tomorrow my school has three days' leave. I want to go to Miss He. Do you want to come with me?'

I answered, 'Wait until I have prayed, to see how the Lord leads.'

I went upstairs straight away, and when I had finished praying I combed my hair. Then the Lord said to me, 'Go and be baptised!'[9]

As far as I was concerned, I really had good reason to refuse this. (1) When Miss Yu Cidu returned to Shanghai from Fujian, she passed through Baiyatan[10] and was baptised at Miss He's place. When I heard about it I was very dissatisfied, thinking it a real pity that after all her good work she had to listen to man's words and get baptised. No matter what, I did not agree. Oh, hateful me! I spoke of that which I myself did not know. And now the Lord wanted me to do what I didn't agree with and had criticised. (2) I had already been baptised when I was young. (3) I had heart disease. At this time there was an unceasing battle in my heart. I saw what Matthew's Gospel said in verse 3:17, that when the Lord Jesus came up out of the water a voice from heaven said, 'This is my beloved Son in whom I am well pleased.' He had already been on the earth for thirty years, but only after His baptism did heaven speak forth. This matter is very important. I also remembered that when I myself was saved, I promised the Lord that I wanted to carry out His will obediently and was willing even to give my life – so now, how dare I not go?

---

[9] That is, by immersion.

[10] Margaret Barber lived at Baiyatan, or White Teeth Rock, near Mawei, opposite Pagoda Anchorage.

I straight away called Watchman and said, 'I have decided to go to Miss He, and moreover I want to be baptised.'

He answered immediately, 'I also am going for baptism.'

My second son, Huaizu, said he wanted to go also, so the mother and two sons, three of us, without any previous arrangement, went together to be baptised.

When we arrived at Miss He's house she was out. There was only Miss Liu keeping house. She asked me, 'What have you come for?'

I said, 'When Miss He comes home I will say.'

After a little while Miss He and Miss Li came back. As soon as they saw me they said, 'Mrs Ni, peace! Have you come for something special today?'

I then said, 'Yes, the Lord wants me to come and be baptised.'

Miss He again asked me, 'Through whom did the Lord come and tell you this?'

I said, 'It was through nobody. After I was praying the Lord Himself told me.' I then told her one by one all the experiences I had been through.

The three of them together praised the Lord and said, 'Miss Yu passed through here and told us what you had been through, and before the presence of God we have earnestly prayed for you, that you not only might be saved, but also be a useful vessel of the Lord in whom He delights. We all saw we ought to tell you the truth about baptism; without submission to this step it cannot be. For this reason we went to Fuzhou twice to look for you, but did not meet. We were certainly clear that you ought to take this step, but why didn't we meet? We then asked the Lord for the reason. He very clearly gave us to know that He didn't want us to come and tell you, but He wanted to tell you Himself. It is true, we have heard with our own ears how the Lord has led you to come. May we all kneel down together in prayer and thank our heavenly Father for His grace and work.'

This was the first time they had prayed together with me. Then it was decided to baptise on the Lord's Day, Easter Sunday.

On the morning of the Lord's Day my frequent illness suddenly returned, and I told Miss He. She said, 'You will see, perhaps we can alter the day.'

Thank the Lord, He within me had unspeakable power, and I said, 'Don't be afraid. This is Satan's hindrance. I would rather die in the will of God than live in my own will.' Oh! This is a wonderful thing: how could a selfish person like me speak like this? This was done by God Himself, and so we went to the baptism.

When we arrived I prayed, saying, 'Oh God, when Your beloved Son our Lord was baptised, the heavens opened for Him because You were well pleased with Him. If You are also pleased with me, please open the heavens for me also.'

Truly God was gracious to me and deigned to hear my prayer. That day it rained a little and the sky was dark, but just as my baptism was over and I came up out of the water the heavens also opened for me: just in that one minute the sun came out and shone brightly on us. That day I knew that as the Father was pleased with the Lord Jesus, so He was also pleased with us. Watchman and Huaizu were also baptised the same day. Miss He then gave me a word of Scripture: 'Out of Egypt have I called my son' (Matthew 2:15).

On Tuesday morning we returned home, because every Tuesday afternoon at two o'clock Pastors Huang and Xi directed Bible study in my home. When we arrived home they were already there, and seeing me hurriedly come in from outside they asked, 'Where did you go?'

I said, 'I've been to Miss He to be baptised.'

They were mightily displeased and told me I had sinned a great sin. I did not believe it and asked them to identify the point wherein I had sinned. I told them how God had led me and how, after baptism, I had experienced unspeakable peace and joy, how God had answered my prayer and how the heavens had opened for me. They said my sin was, first, that I lightly esteemed my baptism by the church; second, that I also lightly esteemed my parents having me baptised; third, that I also dared to overthrow baptism in the name of Jesus: my sin was very terrible. I was immature and, listening to this, began to fear. Quickly I went into the room, knelt down on both knees and said to the Lord, 'Oh Lord, pity my stupid ignorance. These two pastors have been in the church for many years; they have today condemned me and truly pained me. What is this matter? Please give me a word to comfort my heart.'

Oh, our loving Lord is truly a compassionate Lord, and gave me Romans 11:7. 'What then? That which Israel sought for, he obtained not, but the elect obtained it, and the rest were hardened.' Although I am stupid, according to the words, I already fully understood the meaning. It is not by man that everybody receives illumination, but those whom God has chosen can obtain His illumination.

I came out of the room happily. They asked me, 'How about it?' I then showed them the scripture the Lord had given me. They looked at each other, and showed that they were amazed, and everybody was silent. Then the Bible study began.

After this God prepared somebody to rent my house. I then moved and went to live at Cangqian mountain. The Bible study class was dropped. Soon afterwards Miss Pan, of the Methodist Society, invited me to go again to Fuzhou for meetings. When I came back the God of Glory appeared to me and wanted me to leave every kind of work, such as president of the Necessity of Virtue Society, leader of the Prayer Group, vice-president of the Benefit Society, leader of the Moral Culture Group, etc., to serve Him only.

I felt very strange about this and asked the Lord to explain and lead more clearly. Our patient Father then put a thought within me saying it was like a gardener in weary toil all his life not getting any fruit to offer to his master; also like a door-keeper when the thief had already got in and he didn't know it; also like a washer-man who couldn't bring what he had washed before his master for him to wear; also like an old woman who burnt the rice, and although the rice was cooked, her master couldn't eat it. Oh my Lord, after I had these thoughts I really didn't know what to do for the best, for previously I only knew how to exhort others to work with the utmost effort, and didn't know how to leave activities and come and serve God only.

I hurried to Pastor Wang Ganhe to tell him what the Lord had manifested to me, and how He wanted me to stop all activities and serve Him only. He answered, saying, 'There is absolutely nothing of the kind. Man can only serve God zealously, with the utmost effort. I have never heard of ceasing work to serve God. If you are too enthusiastic, your nerves will suffer. If you see I am not worthy to be a pastor, I will let you come and be pastor.'

As he spoke to me like this I could only be unwilling to answer, and took my leave. I repented and went to see him, but not only did it not solve my problem, it added many difficulties. Hateful, stupid me: thinking Chinese people wouldn't do, I went to look for a foreigner.

After a few days I went to look for Miss Pei and told her what I had been through. She said to me very quietly, 'Did you think you wanted to do what John Wesley did? Most people didn't want what he did and they persecuted him, so he was successful. Now all of us in the church want you to work – why do you want to do something besides? Oh, this is not an easy matter!

'Let me tell you a true story. There was somebody who loved the Lord very much who wanted to work zealously as a freelance, so he left the Methodist Church and worked with all his might. One day he saw a garden beside a road surrounded by a bamboo fence. Inside *zhen zhu mi*[11] had been sown. Outside the fence he also saw a *zhen zhu mi* plant which had grown much more healthy and good looking than those inside the fence. He was impressed by the thought that the *zhen zhu mi* plants inside the fence were like church members, and this plant outside the fence was himself. He was very pleased because of this and thought that to leave the church was quite right. But after a little while he passed that way again and saw that the plant outside the fence had already been eaten by a pig. He was then aroused to understand his failings, and immediately

---

[11] Literally 'true pearl grain'.

returned to the church. If you do not heed what I say today, you will also come to that day.'

But I did not in the least understand within. It was as though she was speaking to a stone, and we parted unhappily.

After I got home I lived a confused life for several months. When it came to leaving the church, not one person agreed. Perhaps it was wrong. Yet if I thought about not leaving the church, I was inwardly distressed as though there were some matter of disobedience separating me from God. Oh, this kind of life is very bitter! I passed the days vacillating from morning to evening.

One day I happened to take out from a pile of books a leaflet written by Miss Shi of the Church of England Society, the subject of which was a bamboo. An owner spent much thought and work on nourishing a bamboo in his garden, waiting for it to grow fully. He got up early every day and watered it himself; at times when there were dead leaves or insects he very gently took them off; his love for it never came short in the smallest details. Before long it grew to be the most beautiful and lovable tree in the garden. It was very grateful to its master for the period of his tending it in grace, and a season of grace had a recompense.

One day the master came up to it and said softly, 'Oh, my dear bamboo, you have grown so beautiful and lovable. It was truly not in vain that I once took great pains over you. Now I am thinking of using you, I don't know whether you will be willing or not.'

It answered very quickly, 'Master, I truly want to repay your grace in nourishing me. How could I be unwilling?'

The master said, 'But before I can use you, it is necessary to chop you down.'

The bamboo did not wait for the master to finish speaking and said quickly, 'Oh master, this is too hard! Hitherto I was the only honourable one in the garden because I grew taller than all the other trees, and my eyes viewed everything else with contempt. Now if you cut me down I shall be horizontal on the ground, down beneath them, and from there I will never lift up my head again. Master, I will agree to anything else, only this thing I cannot.'

The master said, 'If I do not first cut you down from your natural place and lay you flat on the ground, I cannot use you. Please remember, formerly when I nurtured you for a time, what was the purpose of it?'

The bamboo, because it wanted to repay the master's grace, therefore repressed the pain and answered the master, saying, 'May your will be done.' The master forthwith took a sharp axe and cut it down, laying it on the ground. While it was being cut down, its pain was incomparable, but because it wanted to recompense grace, it endured it willingly.

The next day the master went to it again and said, 'Oh, my dear bamboo, now I want to cut off all your leaves, then I can use you. I don't know whether you are willing or not.'

The bamboo listened, got worried and answered, 'Master, this demand is unnecessarily harsh. I have already been cut down to the ground by you and cannot loftily rise up again and stand erect. All I can boast of now is these purplish-blue leaves. Can it be that your hard heart will also take away my only remaining beauty? Master, leave me alone, and let me answer to another demand of yours.'

The master shook his head and said, 'If your leaves are not cut off, I cannot use you. Please remember, when I formerly nourished you for a season, what was the purpose of it?'

The bamboo, because it wanted to repay the master's grace, no matter how, restrained its tears and nodded assent. The master then took a pair of shears and cut off all its leaves, and stripped it of its boasted beauty.

After another day had passed the master came again and said to it, 'Oh, my dear bamboo, now I want to do away with all the twigs on you, and afterwards I will be able to use you.'

After the bamboo heard this, it wailed, saying, 'Master, you have already cut off my leaves; if you further slice off the twigs I shall then become a most ugly and slender long pole such as has never been before. Looking like this, what likeness to a bamboo shall I have any more? Master, this kind of thing cannot be other than very unreasonable.'

The master said, 'If I do not pare off your twigs, I cannot use you. Please remember, when I formerly nourished you for a season, what was my purpose?'

The bamboo was caught between the two difficulties, but, moved by the master's grace, it could only be obedient. The master used a knife and sliced off all its twigs, making it a bare and naked bamboo pole.

On the fourth day the master came again and said to it, 'Oh, my dear bamboo, this is my last demand. I now want to use a chisel and tunnel a way through each one of your joints. After that I can use you.'

The bamboo howled and wailed before the master and said, 'Master, my root is already cut, my leaves are already cut off, my twigs are already done away with. How is it you still want to tunnel through my inside joints? This is unnecessarily cruel. Moreover, there are innumerable trees in the garden – why do you let them off and every time treat me harshly?'

The master replied, 'Although there are many trees in the garden, I love you the most, so I chose you to be a suitable vessel for me. Oh, bamboo! Without me chiselling through your joints, I cannot use you. Otherwise I had better place you for ever on the ground. Thus the suffering on the three former occasions will be in vain.'

The bamboo conferred with the master over and over again, but although the master loved it he had no way to avoid the pain. The bamboo, because it thought of the master's grace, then complied with his desire. So the master chiselled through each joint and made it a hollow tube. He then picked it up: one end he connected with the spring and the other end went through into the middle of a field, making the ground fertile through irrigation, and bearing much produce.

At the end of this leaflet there was a question: 'Oh, believers, are you willing to be God's tube of flowing, living water?' My heart was seized by this sentence. It suddenly dawned upon me and was clear. Regardless of everything, I then told Watchman all I had seen and wanted to do, and asked him to write a letter for me to the superintendent of the Methodist Society. He assented and wrote for me.

After the letter had been sent, everyone was truly amazed. Never had there been such a thing in the Methodist Church in Fujian. They said to me that only those who sinned were expelled; how was it that anyone should want to resign because of zeal? It certainly could not be so. From then on some regarded me as proud, some regarded me as having gone the wrong way, and some came to seek me with every kind of criticism, censure and ridicule. Oh Lord, You are unfathomable by men, and have done to this small worm that which man cannot fathom. Your grace is truly most great.

In the three churches the daily subject matter for discussion and criticism was Mrs Ni's leaving the church. Added to this was a group who said they loved me and exhorted me to return, and invited me to meals to enlighten me, for they feared that danger and trouble were before me. Oh, loving Lord, if You had not kept me, I would soon have left the right road.

One day I told all these circumstances to Miss He, and she said to me, 'Satan's attacks you perhaps can know and, trusting the Lord, stand firm. Satan's smiling face I fear you would yield to.' She truly had vision to know me. I thanked her for her prayers, enabling me to stand firm to this day. God knows that I am one who could not stand the praise of men, and because of this I have met opposition and attack all along the way.

Not only was it like this from without, but it was like this in the Ni home also. If anybody told the Ni family how I ministered outside and how God used me, my family would gather a few girls together to grin sarcastically and say a whole lot that even non-Christians would not dare to say. One day somebody told my mother-in-law that because of my preaching many repented and were moved, and she answered, 'She can bark,' meaning that she regarded me as a dog. When I heard it, although I did not say anything, actually I was hurt. Now I know that I am not even as good as a dead dog, so what does it matter?

▲ Bridge of Ten Thousand Ages, Fuzhou

▲ Trams and rickshaws, Shanghai, 1932

▲ Margaret Barber (standing) with Margaret Ballord at Pagoda Anchorage, 1928

▲ Watchman Nee, 1939

▲ Rooftop in Shanghai, 1932.
Seated: Dr Yu, Watchman Nee, John Chang, Faithful Luke with delegation of world brethren

▲ Wedding of Watchman Nee and Charity Cheng, 1934. On left, bride-groom's sister (Mrs Ling), mother, brother (Hong-tsu) and father. On right, bride's sister-in-law and brother (Samuel Chang) and eldest sister (Beulah)

▲ Wedding photo of Watchman Nee and Charity

▲ Centre: LIN Heping, Watchman Nee's mother
From Left: NI Guichen, Watchman Nee's first (oldest) sister
Rear Left: NI Guizhen, Watchman Nee's second sister
Rear Right: ZHANG Pinhui (Charity ZHANG), Watchman Nee's wife
Front Right: XU Fengxian, Watchman's brother George's wife

▲ Chinese junks on river

Chapter 6

Before long there arose in the family a big matter, in that my husband built a new house amid much confusion. At first we rented land from a Meiwu local man to begin building. Afterwards the Fuzhou Government Land Control Organisation was established, making all public property in the district belong to the Land Control Organisation. When my husband heard this, he paid out money to the Land Control Organisation and bought it as personal property. This was because the house was already built on the land and if we did not buy it, it could be bought by somebody else first and the house pulled down. The Land Control Organisation not only permitted us to buy, but forthwith gave us a certificate for the property.

With the money already paid and the certificate in his hand, my husband naturally did not pay the monthly rent for the land. Because of this, public anger was aroused and a public accusation was made to the local law court accusing the Land Control Organisation and my husband. They had no way of dealing with the Land Control Organisation, however, so could only attack my husband with all his might.

Inwardly I perceived that this affair was very much to be feared, but my poor husband did not in the least believe it. He said, 'The money is paid, the certificate has arrived. If there is a mistake, it's the Land Control Organisation's mistake. What has it to do with me?'

I immediately urged my husband to leave Fujian for a time, and let me request a man to come forward and adjust the matter. When there was some clarification, then he could come back and finalise the affair. Alas, he firmly held that he was right and was not willing to leave Fuzhou. When the day came that a man arrived at our home to apprehend him, then he went upstairs and asked for the Lord's grace that the matter would pass peacefully. When he came downstairs and I gave him the public document to read, he said, 'The public document doesn't say "apprehend him", but only that "he is required to go to the court". Why be afraid?' Poor man! Because he was too self-confident that he himself was right, he had no fear at all.

One day, when he was walking on the street, he was really arrested. The local bullies took him to the law court with great joy and rejoicing. When this news came to my ears, I altogether blamed my husband for not listening to me; he had brought this on himself. But the Ni family all blamed me, saying that I was unable to cope, and so things had turned out like this. Also in the church there were some who said it was because I had gone the wrong way: this was retribution for leaving the church.

At that time the Fuzhou meeting was very immature and did not know how to help me. Thank the Lord, in the middle of many kinds of difficulties He sent Miss He from Baiyatan to Fuzhou to stay in my home and to go with me into

the city to visit my husband and pray with him and comfort
him. In the law court they treated him with unusual politeness because he had been an overseer in the Maritime Customs, and they gave him not only a special reception room,
but a messenger to serve him. I honestly say that, compared
with him, I suffered much more terribly at home.

Miss He insisted much on waiting at home, prayer, and
quietly seeing what was God's will, but the relatives of the
Ni family all regarded me as very cruel to allow my husband
to suffer and not seek the help of others outside. They said
that if we did not ask somebody, why should they do so?
Because of this they did not do anything except talk about
my whole life, saying how bad and wrong I was; they sat
and criticised, cursed and reviled me with all their might.
Some of what they said was fact, but they added spice: some
was forged and trumped up. There is a saying that although
the tiger is savage, it does not eat its own offspring, but my
accusers said I threw my own fourth daughter down from
the third storey to kill her. Oh my God, You are omniscient.
You know I haven't done anything like this, or even
thought of such a thing.

One day, because I was being oppressed, I thought to
redress my grievance, but before I went I first prayed before
God, saying, 'Oh God, I want to exonerate myself and teach
them a lesson because what they said was altogether false;
it was fabricated.' Unexpectedly, just as I stopped praying,
God's word came, from Song of Songs 2:2: 'As a lily among
thorns, so is my love among the daughters.' This gave me a
little understanding about the position of us Christians in
the world: although surrounded by thorns, God wants us to
be like lilies among the thorns to show forth our beauty and

distinctiveness. If we are surrounded by lilies, our beauty and distinctiveness cannot be seen. God also gave me to see that if the lilies and thorns collide and contend, only the lilies are injured and broken, but the thorns are just as before, so what benefit could I obtain?

I also remembered that Psalm 37:1 says, 'Do not fret because of evil-doers.' Verse 8 also says, 'Do not fret yourself into doing evil.' Because of this I did not go. The Bible tells us, 'Pray in all things.' If a Christian can pray in all things, he will not sin so much. If I had not first prayed on this occasion and had God's hindrance, and had gone as I had first intended, I do not know how great would have been the injury to God's name. May God have compassion on us, that we pray in all things.

At that time Satan was violent, attacking within and without, and truly would have cast me off and fought against me. If it had not been for the Almighty protecting me, one like me as weak as water, I do not know where I would soon have gone. It is just as our brother Paul said, 'We are pressed on every side, yet not straightened, perplexed, yet not despairing, pursued, yet not forsaken, smitten down, yet not destroyed.'

In the end God was gracious and sent a brother to us who said a relative of his was a barrister and could help in the conclusion of my husband's case. So I went into the city to see the barrister and prayed to God to give me wisdom to speak well. He truly did not decline to hear my cry. When I saw the barrister I took less than five minutes to tell my husband's case clearly from beginning to end. The barrister was very surprised and said it was rare to find a woman speaking so simply, clearly, eloquently and magnanimously.

With all his heart he was pleased to help; there was not the least difficulty. In a few days he said to me, 'Tomorrow afternoon you may take a carriage and go and receive your husband.' It was true. When the time arrived I received my husband back again, and the expenditure was not great. Is this not God bestowing compassion and grace upon whom He wills to do so? So I know that, apart from God, nothing is to be trusted. I also with full heart thank my dear sister Miss He, who in my time of difficulty showed sympathy in standing together with me. The Lord truly remembered my weakness and sent His handmaiden to strengthen me. My God is one who should receive our thanks and praise. Amen.

Before long, regardless of my reputation, I often went to see my mother-in-law and talked to her of the grace and light God had given me. The result was that God really got her, and her attitude towards me changed a lot. Not only so, she often sent me good things to eat and specially commissioned the servant to say that I had many children in the home, and I was very busy, so I was to eat the things myself and not share them with the children. If for a few days I did not go and see her, she would send somebody to see me as she was afraid I was sick. One day, when my eldest son graduated from high school, she gave me ten dollars to have a gown made for him to wear. Oh, all this shows clearly that she now loved me. For nearly a year and a half I often went to see her, and she liked me to mention the things of the Lord.

One day my fifth sister-in-law said to me, 'Your mother-in-law now loves you very much. If you don't come the old lady is anxious about you, and it is all because of what the

Lord has done in you over these recent years.' Inwardly I bowed and acknowledged it and gave the glory to God. My eldest sister-in-law also once said to me, 'Mother's attitude towards you has completely changed.' I just smiled and did not answer.

Thank God, while she was on the earth over another year, there was love and fellowship between her and her daughters-in-law. Before long I went to South-east Asia to preach the gospel, so I was not beside her when she left the world. Afterwards, when I came back, everybody said to me that my mother-in-law had hoped I would be able to get home, but it was God who decided and I dared not say anything. Nonetheless, I had a part in her burial at the cemetery, and at a memorial service in the home they also insisted that I took responsibility. I could only accept it for the Lord's sake.

When the funeral affairs were over, the grinding of family hardships continued uninterrupted. Because my natural gifts were utterly bad and God's love and grace boundless, he especially sought me out to show forth His sympathy and great power for men to see how compassionate a God He is.

My third son Xuanzu and my eldest daughter Guichen were brought up in my mother's home. Out of love, my parents were originally willing to bear this heavy load for us, but afterwards, because of this mutual dependence for livelihood, mother and daughter became great enemies. Oh my God, You should be praised! 'All things work together for good to them that love God.' This word can never be changed. My parents were aged, so it was natural that they loved their granddaughter. Because they loved too much and did not correct, however, they allowed this to happen.

So every time I went home or they came to my home, reproof was useless. But know that to use man's strength and pray in the flesh is not the least use. Not only can they not reform, but my own daughter came to be to me a wicked go-between with my mother's family.

Before I was saved it was all right, because gambling and cinemas pacified the mother's heart, but after I was saved these things were naturally cut off. My mother at first hoped that I was only temporarily affected; she said that before long I would recover my usual behaviour and, as before, go with her into the pleasures of sin. How could she know that the Lord Jesus, having truly saved me out of the midst of sin, would never let me gamble etc. with her again? On the one hand this made her surprised that my change was so thorough, and on the other hand it made her hate Miss Yu. She did not know what method she had used to make me completely turn to the Lord Jesus Christ at this stage. Even when I bought things for the old lady to eat, she would not eat any of them, and she was afraid I would preach the gospel to her. Because of this I very seldom went to my mother.

My poor third son – because I desired comfortable circumstances for him and did not bring him up myself, it caused him to stray. He joined the Iron and Blood Volunteers, the Dare-to-Die Corps and such organisations, reputedly to save the nation, but really he evaded study and just played around. Finally he was killed.[12]

Oh God, this was all my sin, and apart from seeking Your forgiveness, what can I say?

---

[12] In an accident or uprising.

After my third son died, the voice of cursing and railing such as mankind cannot bear began on all sides. God was my only refuge. When I sang and praised God, people regarded me as having no feelings. My son was dead, yet I could sing and be happy. Actually I reproached and hated myself, and had no leg to stand on. I could only flee to the presence of God and get a little comfort; otherwise I would have committed suicide.

Not long afterwards my father became ill. As soon as the news came, I went back immediately. We both wept bitterly when I saw my dear aged father with paralysis, half his body immobile. He said to me, 'You pray for me. If I can get better, the two of us, father and daughter, will go preaching together.' When I was praying to Father God, He very clearly gave me to know that this sickness would not be healed. I told him that if the sickness was not cured it didn't matter; salvation was the big question. From that day I began to tell my father the essential points of the gospel. Thank God, He saved him. He was thoroughly saved.

When Miss He and Miss Liu went to see him he said to them, 'I was a prodigal, but now I have come home.' And, 'I am Lot. God sent an angel to save me out of Sodom and Gomorrah.' Then with his hand he pointed to me, saying, 'She is the angel God sent to save me.' He also said, 'All that I have done in my life has been vain with the exception that I brought her up, because God used her to bring saving grace to me so that I can go to heaven.' While he spoke, his satisfied eyes looked on me. Oh my God, my Lord, You ought to be praised. My thanksgiving and worship be unto the only ever-living true God and the Lamb who was slain, our Lord Jesus Christ for ever. Amen. He also sang a hymn:

'Grace has an ever open door. . .' As he sang, he was full of faith, peace and joy.

Once I took Mr John Wang to his home to see the old man. Mr Wang asked my father, 'Venerable sir, are you saved?'

He smiled a little but did not speak, and sang in a low voice a chorus instead of an answer: 'Glory in the utmost, holy court in heaven; eternally secure, never will be destroyed; door of precious pearl, walls of gold and jade, I will there arrive and never perish.'

Mr Wang immediately said, 'He very clearly is saved. As he sang the chorus we could sense life.' So we dispersed quite happy.

One day he asked me to pray that the Lord would take him away quickly. It is true, the condition of his illness at that time became critical, and friends and relatives who lived at a distance were informed. When they knew, it was said that it would be best to ask God to be merciful and not take him until after the wedding of my eldest brother's son, who was to be married the next day. So we prayed again, and his sickness slowly became a little better, until four days after the wedding, when he peacefully left this world. His dying wish that my mother would be saved he entrusted to me, hoping that the whole family would meet in heaven.

When it was near the time of my father's funeral, the Methodist board sent a letter inviting me to preach the gospel at the women's meeting on the Monday. After I had prayed I felt I should go, so I responded. I also knew that my father's funeral was on the Tuesday and for this reason all the more decidedly wished to go. Unexpectedly, the day of my father's funeral was suddenly changed to Monday. After

I heard the news I did not know what to do for the best. Miss Liu was staying in my home and made a suggestion, saying, 'Ask somebody to substitute for you.' I agreed to this plan, but running all over the place, I could not find anyone willing to substitute for me. I could only ask God to show me how this matter could be arranged. God then gave me a verse of Scripture, Luke 9:60. Jesus said, 'Let the dead bury their dead, but go then and publish abroad the kingdom of God.'

After I got this news I could only go and see my mother and say to her, 'On Monday I have to go and preach the gospel and cannot come and escort Father to the grave.'

My mother, when she heard this news, truly could not stop her anger. Fire came from her heart and she said to me, 'If that is so, I will hang myself for you to see what your preaching has accomplished. You haven't any human principles; what can you say about heavenly principles? Your father loved you the most, all his life; you think and see, could you face him unashamed? I am a concubine, and am I not extremely laughable to your two brothers and sister? You can preach at any time, but your father's funeral is once in your lifetime. Moreover, many pastors will go and escort the coffin. Can it be that your belief in Jesus is much more profound than theirs, much more special? You must go; certainly you must go.'

There was reason in everything she said, but my spirit within did not flow. If I was not to go, my grief was more than I could speak. I could only kneel down again and pray, and the impression I received was the same as before. Immediately the Lord said, 'Let the dead bury their dead, but go then and publish abroad the kingdom of God.' I, who could not bear it, was pulled in two directions, but I set my heart on obeying God. I also feared the defamation by others and so again knelt down and prayed as before, but the result was very different from the previous times. It was as though God took no notice of me. So I got up very fearfully and definitely obeyed God, willing to pay any price to seek the Lord's pleasure.

My mother sent somebody to ask me to go, but I said I would rather die, and did not go. He then said, 'The sedan chair is prepared and your name is labelled on it. What shall we do?'

I answered, 'Take a big stone and put it in the chair and carry it.' They could only do as I had said, because there was no alternative.

Although my mother was extremely angry, she did not hang herself after all, for God Himself took responsibility to glorify His name. My responsibility was to obey God and please Him, for to obey is better than sacrifice (1 Samuel 15:22). In this I especially want to mention how God's leading can never be wrong. On the day my father was buried I went into the city to preach the gospel of the kingdom of God, and the carriage had to pass my mother's home. I just told the carriage man to let down all the blinds, both going and coming back. The ministry that day was particularly strong, and many people were affected.

God did much more beyond this. At this time my older brother did not belong to the Lord. My father was a businessman, and most of those he traded with were heathen men. On these occasions the eldest son or eldest brother naturally takes responsibility for funeral affairs. When the coffin came out of the door, somebody had employed a

Taoist priest to offer things to the dead all along the way until they came to the place where the coffin stopped. Mr Wang Zai's father particularly wanted to watch how I would behave at this time, but when he did not see me, he hurried to my sedan chair and looked inside. Then he realised it was right that I was not there at the burial ground, and he was astonished beyond belief at God's acts. When the time came for us to go to Guling hill resort in the summer, he told me what he had done.

A few days after my father died, I related to him the circumstances of my father's salvation, and asked him, on behalf of my husband, to write a pair of scrolls to honour my father. He began to write in my presence: 'In the last five minutes he recovered faith; we dare to say he went to heaven's kingdom. He trusted the precious blood of the cross; wholeness speaks of Taishan as ruined.'[13] I also particularly preached the gospel to him, and heard that he was saved.

On this occasion, when God did not allow me to escort the funeral, He had His own good intention. First, God wanted to preserve my consecrated life as holy, that I should not be infected by the unclean, for He chose me as His handmaiden to wait upon Him and serve Him. Second, that unbelievers might see God's acts. Third, that I might see His faithfulness and ability to keep His own, provided we obey Him. So from the heart I say, 'God is worthy to be worshipped; may honour and power be to Him unto all ages. Amen.'

On the second day after my father's funeral I went home

---

13 Taishan is a mountain near Jinan, worshipped as a god.

very early to see my mother. There was not one person in the house who was willing to regard me, but I took away the Bible and hymn book which my father always used, as a remembrance. As to my father's property and goods, they did not give me even a little. How good this was! Oh God, this was Your kindness. From this time many of my mother's family looked upon me as the greatest of wicked sinners. Those in the church looked upon me all the more as a hypocritical Pharisee. As to myself, I wondered what this business was all about. How beloved other Christians are: they have a good reputation and are respected by others. Me? I always came up against criticism and reviling from many people, who regarded my life as strange (Psalm 71:7). Before one wave was quiet, another one came.

Because of this I took these problems and put them before my eldest son, Watchman. His answers were, 'Mother, (1) we are all specially bad people. (2) God has in grace specially called us. (3) You must be specially pruned. (4) God wants to specially use you. (5) You will receive a special reward.' I then added, (6) the devil will get special shame. (7) God will get special glory. These few sentences for the most part I have seen to be factual. Hallelujah, the Lord is worthy to be thanked!

I happened to go home one day and see my mother. She pretended not to know me. The family regarded me as refuse, even showing openly that they were not willing to see me, and I could do nothing about it. A few years later my mother's family suddenly telephoned to say she was dangerously ill. As soon as I received the telephone message I went home with my husband and sons and daughters to see my mother. Under these circumstances, when my mother saw me, she said, 'What have you come for? Don't speak of that.' She meant that she did not want me to speak about believing in the Lord. She entertained us confusedly, and after we had eaten she said, 'Go home.' So I could only bow my head and return with my husband and children.

On arriving home my heart was distressed like a burning fire, so I went to look for Mr John Wang. It was good that Mr Miao Shaoxun (Simon Meek) was there also and we all knelt down together in prayer. When we had finished I went immediately to my mother-in-law's home to ask my second sister-in-law to pray about this. She answered, 'Let the unrighteous be unrighteous still, and let the righteous be righteous still.' Although she spoke like this, inwardly I did not in the least concur, and I went home and solely waited before God in this matter. The Bible says, 'They that wait for me shall not be ashamed.' Oh my Father, You truly are the God worthy to receive praise and worship; as You say, so it is fulfilled.

God said to me that my mother certainly could be saved, but I must go and see her again. But I had a little doubt in my heart: how could she be influenced with conditions like this between mother and daughter? I did not disbelieve that she could be saved, but I thought it was very unsuitable for God to use me. But no matter how, inwardly I was conscious that God purposely would use me to go, because there was no way of finding another to go. So I could only answer God, 'I am willing to go; please You Yourself do the work.' And God answered that He Himself would work.

I got up early in the morning, combed my hair and washed, and went to see my mother, arriving there in just five minutes. When she saw me she said, 'What have you come again for?'

I said, 'I have come for your salvation.'

Then neither of us spoke, and after a little while her sickness broke out again; that sorrowful condition truly was enough to make the hardest of hearts show sympathy. But I could not sympathise. On the contrary, my heart was full of joy so that my face was covered with a smile. When she saw me like this, she was moved with anger and said, 'You haven't human principles; where are your heavenly principles?'

I said, 'You are not at all afraid of everlasting suffering in hell: what does this brief suffering amount to?'

Just this one sentence of mine aroused her and she immediately said, 'Like this, what can I do?'

I said, 'There are no conditions except to kneel down and pray to the Lord, and He will surely save you.'

Oh our God, it was Your work, it is You who are to be praised! My mother then turned herself to get up, and with her eyes looking at me she gave me her hand to pull her up. I immediately pulled her up. She said to me, 'I don't know how to pray.'

I said, 'Never mind. I will pray a sentence, and you repeat it after me.'

This was the first time mother and daughter with one mind prayed together before God. She heard me pray a sentence, then she prayed a sentence. When we had finished she said, 'That is my heart's desire.'

I then went on praying for her. I made a request and she said, 'I thus request.' I made another request and she said again, 'I thus request.' When I had finished she said again,

'That is my heart's desire.' Our hearts both had fresh joy and carried a taste of heaven.

I then asked my mother, 'Will you go to heaven and not be cast into hell?'

She smiled all over her face and said, 'I will go to heaven and not be cast into hell.'

I said, 'How will it be in the end?'

She then repeated the Lord's Prayer and Hymn 43, verse 2: 'Jesus loves me, He who died heaven's happy gate to open wide; He will wash away my sin, save me in the eternal gate. *Chorus*: Truly Jesus loves me, the Bible clearly says.' She sang in sincerity and truth, causing those who heard to touch God's life; God is worthy to receive worship.

She also took my hand and rather shamefacedly said, 'What about my previous treatment of you?'

I said, 'I have forgiven you a good while ago, don't speak about that.'

She wanted me to comb her hair and I immediately did it for her. She also wanted me to wash her, and I was very pleased to do so. She saw that I perspired all over on her behalf and felt very concerned and said, 'Your clothes are soaked with perspiration, what had you better do?' I shook my head to show it was unimportant. I just wanted her to be comfortable, and it was all right.

She also showed that she was satisfied with what I had done for her. She called me, saying, 'You must sit by my side because I feel very happy when you are sitting with me.'

I answered, 'This is only for a little while. When you get to heaven you will be for ever with the Lord, sitting at His feet, and nothing could be better than that.'

She closed her eyes and in a moment opened them again

and with a little smile said, 'Yes.' Then she asked me, 'Could we pray a little more?'

I asked her, 'What is it you want to pray about?'

She answered, 'Ask God if He wants to heal me to do so, but if He wants me to go to heaven that He will take me soon from this world, because when the illness occurs the pain is incomparable.'

I then said, 'All right.'

So mother and daughter for the second time knelt down and prayed together. When we got up I sat her on the bed. Just then somebody brought food in. She saw there was a big bowl of autumn cucumber soup and said, 'I want to eat.'

When I took the soup, somebody waiting on her called saying, 'It is nearly twelve o'clock, when she ought to take her medicine.' She then took the medicine and put it to her mouth, and I took the soup to give her to drink. When she was taking it she could not swallow, and she passed away peacefully to the Lord Jesus, who gave His life and shed His blood for us.

When she passed on in this way, not only did I not weep, but I was truly happy, and thanked the Lord for calling her from the world. Many people regarded me as unfilial, not loving my mother, and thought that was why I did not cry. I could only patiently endure it. If I cried it would certainly be pretence, and I would be all the more distressed. I felt that to endure oppression was very much better than to pretend.

On the day of my mother's burial I got up very early and very respectfully escorted her to the grave. Naturally the pomp of the funeral affairs did not come up to a tenth of my father's, but I thank God that He fulfilled the desire of my father's heart and mine that she would be saved, and we can meet again in the heavenly city. What manner of grace is this! God is worthy to be praised.

Chapter 7

When the sufferings of home were eased a little, the suffering of illness came down again in that I got high blood pressure, buzzing in the ears, inflammation of the throat, suppuration, swollen nose, indistinct vision every day, headache every day, palpitation of the heart, acidity of the stomach, and beriberi with swollen feet and difficulty in walking. The more sick I was, the more corpulent I became, with not the least bit of strength, and I could not get up much. Who could understand suffering like this?

At this time the family income was particularly limited. Income was insufficient for expenditure, because my husband had already left the Maritime Customs and was not working. My husband had invested money in the fishing industry and water supply industry, and had also lent money to people and paid for his own life insurance. Although a lot of money was put out, it not only did not earn money back, but carried heavy debts. In all these things God wanted me to go through lack of money, and a sick body without even the means to call a doctor. My husband was concerned neither about the home nor my sickness.

One day, when I was sick nigh unto death, I definitely decided to call a doctor. It was not at all easy to send somebody to call the doctor for an early visit. The fee was ten dollars. After he had seen me he wrote a prescription. After my husband saw the prescription he wanted to go himself to buy the medicine, being afraid that one of the children would not be clear about it. I thanked him very much for troubling like this. But who would have thought it? By twelve o'clock he had not returned; by six o'clock in the evening he had not come, and he did not return until ten o'clock at night. He came to my room and said, 'Are you a little better today?'

I saw he had completely forgotten and didn't mention buying the medicine, and I could not help saying, 'Not very well. I've been waiting for you to come back with the medicine to take.'

But he asked me, 'What medicine?'

Enduring the pain, I told him about the doctor's call in the morning. Then he remembered and told me that as soon as he went out of the door he met a friend who took him off on a boat trip to enjoy the coolness, because the weather was hot enough to make one faint. I was too angry to say a word, and did not sleep all night. What about him? It was as though it was nothing to do with him. Oh God, this is Your hand adding heavy pressure on me. What can I say in return?

There is an ancient saying: 'If you are long on a sick bed, you have no loyal son.' This is a true saying. Once the servant brought food to my room, and at the time I was in a sweet sleep. The servant could not bear to wake me, so simply put the food down there. When I awoke it was already cold, so I could only call my daughter in a loud voice to come and heat the food again, because the servant had gone to buy vegetables. I was shocked when she said audaciously, 'You are always sick. Who has the time to come and serve you? I want to study and I'm not coming.' After I heard these words all I could do was to hold the cold food in my mouth until it was warm, and then swallow it.

'Oh my God,' I thought, 'today I am finished; this situation of my own daughter opposing me like this is all permitted by You.' I hadn't the strength to deal with her. Apart from remaining silent and restraining my anger, I had no alternative. In addition, there was the financial hardship. I wanted to buy fruit and things to eat, but felt it was difficult to speak. But Abba Father God, You saw all these conditions, and remembered. Just when I could no longer bear it, a sister in the Lord came and took up my Bible, and put eleven dollars inside. She thought I was a rich person, but on the other hand she was moved, so she secretly put the money inside the Bible. Oh my God, although the sum was not great, it was enough for me to see that You truly cared for me.

Before long the Lord moved Dr Shi Meiyu (Dr Stone) to send a telegram inviting me to go to Shanghai to the Bethel Hospital, which she had opened. After I received the telegram I knew it was God's appointment, so I firmly decided to go. But the home needed somebody to look after the children and my husband could not go with me to Shanghai, so I asked God to provide for me. It was good that Dr Lin Huizhen, who usually did not mix much with people, was able to come and see me and tell me that soon she was going to Shanghai to open a dispensary, and moreover was taking two Fuzhou nurses with her. As soon as I heard this news I knew it was God's plan – nothing better – so I told her my need. She immediately promised that she would look after me all the way, and take me as far as Bethel. With a full heart I thanked the grace of my heavenly Father, and on the same day began to make preparations to go.

At that time my husband did all he could to help by gathering up the luggage, and when the time came he escorted me to the boat. I took a second-class cabin, four people in one room, a doctor and two nurses accompanying a sick person peacefully all the way to Shanghai. Although Dr Stone sent somebody to meet me, we did not meet, and Dr Lin herself hired a taxi to take me to Bethel Hospital. On the boat the doctor and two nurses never came short in the smallest details in caring for me. Is this not the grace of God? God is worthy to be praised, for He was gracious to me, this chief of sinners. I will worship Him for ever. Amen.

When I arrived at Bethel Hospital I received much kindness from both Dr Stone and Miss Hu, who put me in a first-class ward, with nurses to serve me day and night. All the nurses were very good to me, and through me the Lord led some of them to be clearly saved and truly obtain His life. I stayed in the hospital for several months, and not only did not pay for the hospital or medicine, but received many good garments which Dr Stone had had made for me, and she told me they were willing to work with me. But because it was not God's will for it to be arranged thus, we separated, and I went to Hardoon Road and stayed with my eldest son, Watchman. He worked together with several sisters. What he preached was too deep, and I could not understand it, but their life truly brought me to the ground in respect as soon as I saw it. Because I myself came too far short, was not willing to ask questions, and was too proud, I could not receive anything from them. Now, as I think of that time, it was a pity.

I had not stayed long before my son became ill. I myself was sick and had no alternative but to go to Miss Pei's home. She also showed me much love, keeping me there for a week, and herself bought material and made with her own hands a sleeping garment for me. She said, 'Although other people have received many things from me, they don't come up to the sleeping garment I have made for you with my own hand. I shall be sixty years old this year, and I give it to you to commemorate this.'

Before long my illness was severe, and I returned to Bethel Hospital. Dr Stone, as before, treated me very well, and did not change her manner because I had not consented to work with them. As a Christian she was very broad, one truly to be respected. But I was not like that: if there was the least thing not to my liking, my manner and state of mind were not happy, and how shameful this was! The Bible tells us, 'Love bears all things.' Now I see how far short my life at that time was from the beloved goal. Oh my God! On one side I ask You to forgive, and on the other side I ask You to make me run straight towards the goal, and through me glorify Your own holy name. Amen.

I stayed at Bethel Hospital many days. When I was better I went to stay at Hardoon Road again. Although the sickness was healed, I was very weak and had no strength, and could not look after my son very much. At times I forced myself to devote service to him. I always thought he would be grateful for my help to him in sickness and in serving him. Not only did I not get this gratitude, but on the contrary I saw he disliked me increasingly with the days. Because of this I purposely said to his face, 'Now that you are sick in Shanghai, it is fortunate that I am here and can help you. If not, I don't know what would be the result.'

He immediately answered, 'It would be much better if you were not here.'

When I heard this I saw that the true condition of his heart towards me was what I had seen and thought. So I went to the missionary home to look for Miss Liu to see whether or not a foreigner was returning to Fuzhou. It was good that an American, Miss Tao, wanted to go to Fuzhou, but she needed two days before leaving. So I returned to Hardoon Road, and the same day gathered my luggage and moved to Bethel for two nights. Afterwards I went back to Fujian with Miss Tao.

Just as I was leaving I said to my son, 'Since you don't like me being here, it is better that I leave. May we each be happy on our own.' He closed his eyes and did not speak. My heart was cut as with a knife. Although it was so, I dared not tell this matter to Miss Liu or Miss Pei or the friends at Bethel. Even when I got home I did not tell anybody, but my heart was very distressed. It was certain that from now on the affection between mother and son would cease. Hereafter I would only have the affection of brothers and sisters in the Lord. Although I had this thought, how difficult it is for man's natural life to be cut off.

Now I know all this was appointed by God's hand. Soon afterwards I heard that my son was likely to die and my heart was distressed, but I could only commit him to God.

Life and death are with God, and are not my affair. After a few more days news came that he had received God's healing, and I was very happy. He also wrote to me confessing sin and saying that in many ways he had wronged me. When I called to mind his actions, my anger arose again, and I wrote a very stern letter to him enumerating his crimes, not in the least thinking that I was a bad mother and had many bad points in the care of my sons and daughters. Now I know a little, and God is continually helping me to know more.

Chapter 8

In 1932 there were special meetings in Shanghai. My son wrote to my husband asking him to have two hundred chairs made for him at $3 each. My husband was not experienced in these things and wanted me to help him. I immediately got a man to go ahead with the work quickly, because the meetings were to begin on the 7th October.[14] When the chairs were finished I entrusted them to the boatman to take them to Shanghai as required, and gave him $50 for customs dues, etc. But the customs receiver wanted to embezzle this amount and only pay out a few dollars to the Maritime Customs examiner of goods, thinking it would pass with no proper declaration process. It so happened that just that day a foreigner came on the boat to investigate, and seeing our two hundred chairs demanded our customs declaration form. Evasion of taxes was a problem at this time, so he had all the chairs transported into the customs house.

---

[14] Heping has the date wrong here: the meetings began on 7 November 1932 (see Watchman Nee's biography *Against the Tide*, by Angus and Jean Kinnear, revised edition published by Kingsway, 2006).

As soon as this news came it made me so anxious, I truly did not know which way to turn. Apart from God there was no way. After prayer my husband went to the customs house to petition the commissioner with all the facts, and to acknowledge our fault that we were lazy in not going ourselves to declare the customs, and so on. God was gracious to us, and the commissioner was willing to allow us to declare customs immediately and have release, which only cost $35.

At that time Mr John Wang happened to come and see us and we asked him to help us in the matter of transportation. He responded immediately, because the captain of the Wanxing boat was his fellow student. Later brother Xi Zuoh came up from Baiyatan, and the Lord gave me to see that I ought to commission him to clear the two hundred chairs in the customs house and take them for me to the Wanxing boat. I therefore told him everything. Thanks to the grace of the Lord, he carried out everything for me in detail. If the Lord had not taken responsibility, would not our plan have failed? He will not fail, for He is God; I worship Him.

At this time I felt I ought to go to Shanghai to attend the special meetings, and the same day I gathered my luggage. It was good that Mr Zhen Guosan came to see me; he said he had received a letter from Shanghai inviting him to go. I said that although I had not received a letter, inwardly I felt I must go to the meetings. Could we not all go together? At first he was a little uncertain, but afterwards saw the Lord's appointing, and we went together happily. When my third sister-in-law knew that we were going to Shanghai, she wanted to go also as she would have a companion, so my husband escorted the three of us to the Wanxing boat. The first thing I wanted to know was whether the two hundred chairs were on the boat. I did not care about anything else; I walked from one end of the boat to the other, and saw that the chairs were there. Then I thanked God's grace. His faithfulness can be trusted.

On the day our boat was due at Shanghai, a heavy fog suddenly came down and the captain cast anchor. Everybody lost hope that we could reach Shanghai that day. Somebody said that last time a boat was delayed there it stopped a whole day, so we certainly could not reach Shanghai that day. What they said struck my heart, and I said to brother Chen, 'We will pray to God to disperse this fog. Today is the 6th, and the meetings begin tomorrow the 7th, at nine o'clock in the morning. If the boat doesn't arrive, what will we do?' He immediately responded, and we three with one heart and mind besought God to command the fog to disperse. At that moment the weather cleared and in less than five minutes the boat started again. People on the boat all wondered how it had started again. Some said it was all because those few believers in Jesus had prayed, others said it was by chance, others said they saw us praying. Everybody talked about this unceasingly. We three thanked the grace of God.

Before long the captain sent a man asking, 'Are these chairs yours or not? If they are, you must pay $200; $1 for each chair.' These words were as the sound of a loud crash of thunder on a fine day. We had already spent a lot on travelling expenses. We originally thought that with booking first-class cabins it would include the chairs; they didn't occupy much space and could be reckoned as our luggage.

So everybody thought I should see the captain and first mention Mr John Wang and see how he reacted. Second, I was a lady passenger and so with me perhaps he might be a little more polite. And so I went.

Unexpectedly, he showed himself unfriendly when I mentioned Mr Wang, and when I mentioned that it might be better to ask him to come and see him, he showed himself unwilling. I am not one who is willing to be lightly esteemed by others because I ask for favours, so I did not say much more. I went down and told the others the circumstances I had been through, and said that now we had no other way but to pray again. Our dear brother then said he would not pray because he had no faith. In the face of this, we were all silent.

After a moment I felt inwardly that we must pray, so I said, 'Brother, it's all right if you don't pray. If I pray, you just need to say "Amen". Will that be all right?' He thought a moment, then agreed. So we three all knelt down and prayed. As I knelt down I envisaged the chairs we had brought all placed in the meeting room at Hardoon Road, and even saw all the prospects for the meetings the next day. So with great boldness before God's presence I turned prayer into praise, believing that God would certainly carry out the goal before our eyes. Our brother readily joined in saying 'Amen'. When we got up I told him what I had seen, and he continuously nodded his head and thanked God. When the boat neared the shore the captain came to say that he only required $50, and that would do. We immediately agreed to it and gave him $50.

At the wharf we saw that many brothers had come to meet us because of the chairs, but the devil was still not willing to let go of them. When we left the boat the Maritime Customs on their side would not unload the goods that day, because it was too late, and the boat was immediately turning round to go to Pudong. Fortunately brother Hu Zhidang, with several other brothers, stayed on the boat and went to Pudong and there hired a small boat to bring the chairs to the wharf. I gave them the Maritime Customs clearance certificate and they arrived at Hardoon Road with the chairs at eleven o'clock that night. When the chairs arrived, I immediately helped to place them and dust them until I could not do any more.

The next day at nine o'clock the meetings began, and it was the same as I had seen the previous day on the boat. What other people's feelings were during the meetings I did not know. I myself truly had a special taste, a joy which could not be withstood. Oh God, I will regard Your faithfulness as provision. You have treated this child with grace and love. I am both perverse and foolish, but You have a highway and it shall be called the way of holiness. The unclean shall not pass over it; it shall be only for the redeemed to walk in. Though the travellers be fools, they shall not err therein. How reliable this is! I therefore worship before You.

On this occasion the subject was new, and I received a little light and help. When the meetings were ended, brother Zhen Guosan returned with me to Fujian.

Soon afterwards God gave me to see the truth about head-covering. By the Lord's grace I submitted to what previously I had not been able to. I do not know about other people who covered their heads, but for me personally to obey the truth of head-covering, God required me to pay a price. One day a brother came to my home and said that he did not see anything in the head-covering truth. He was a local responsible brother, and wanted me not to cover my head, and he did not permit me to preach about it. He said that since head-covering meant obedience, he invited me that day to show whether or not I would be obedient to the brethren. He promised that he would begin to investigate thoroughly the matter of head-covering, as to whether it agreed with Bible truth, and if it did he would announce to the sisters that they all should cover their heads. By God's grace I answered, 'Let me pray and see; and if this matter is from God, I will certainly obey.'

We dispersed quite happily, but I covered my head at meetings as before. I also put this matter before the Lord in prayer. The answer I received was the story in 1 Kings 13. I was the young prophet; since I had received a command to cover my head, I certainly could not alter God's command because of the old prophet's words. If I did heed his words and not cover my head, I would be punished with death and all the old prophet could do would be to bury me. Because this is not a small matter, there is no way of acting in conformity with man beyond acting in conformity with God.

After a few days this brother came again to my home to ask about the matter of head-covering when in prayer – after all, how about it? I told him the true circumstances, and he was silent. After a little while he said, 'You are only under obligation to obey me; for the rest I am responsible before the presence of God for you.' At that time I truly felt inwardly that this brother was too daring, so I prayed silently to God as to how I should answer him. God then opened my heart and made me understand, and I said, 'On the Lord's Day I will, as before, wear my cap at the meetings. If you have the courage to bear responsibility for me before the Lord, I invite you to come and take it off for me. I am not willing to take it off myself; you must take it off with your own hand, and I certainly will be willing to obey you. If I take it off myself, I must bear the responsibility myself before God.'

He repeatedly said that it only needed me to be willing to take it off myself, and he certainly would bear the responsibility for me before God. I said again, 'Since you are willing to bear responsibility for me, how is it that you do not dare to take it off for me? I see that if I take it off myself I must bear the responsibility of disobedience to God, so if you don't take it off, I will not.' But he said that in the whole church nobody covered their head, and he saw it as unusual. I said if that was so, I would not go to the meetings, lest he should be ill at ease. So from that day I did not go to the meetings. But I asked the Lord daily to be gracious to me and open a way for me.

Before long there were further special meetings in Shanghai, and they sent a telegram to me asking me to be sure to attend. After a few days Huaizu and others sent another telegram inviting my husband and myself to go and arrange Watchman's wedding.[15] As soon as I heard this news I trembled with fear, and thought that in the matter of his marriage I had already been wrong once: how could I touch it again? It is truly said that if matters rest on other people's shoulders all is well; when they are on mine, even

---

[15] To his childhood sweetheart Zhang Pinhui (Charity Chang).

if they are good, they will be spoilt. So I said to my husband,
'You, as father, are head of the home. It will be sufficient for
you to go alone. If I go, there will be a lot of trouble.' I was
truly afraid, and truly not happy to go.

My husband was also not happy to go and feared trouble.
He said, 'I give you full authority. What you do I will
entirely agree with. It will be enough if you go; it is not
necessary for two of us to go.'

While we were thus each making excuses, inwardly I felt
something saying that this was God opening the way out for
me. In prayer the answer came: why don't you go? I then
dared not shirk any more; I could only turn round and
repeatedly exhort my husband to go with me. He forced
himself to prepare the luggage and went, not at all willingly,
as though we knew beforehand that the wedding would
not be well arranged. But on the human side we were his
parents, so we could do nothing but start out for Shanghai.

On arriving at Shanghai we heard a lot of talk going
around about Zhang Meizhen, Pinhui's eldest aunt, who
wanted to make trouble and not allow her niece to marry a
poor preacher, etc. She also used a lot of excessive slander,
attacking my son. Her foolish talk and lies increased with
the days – truly a mystery. I really could not believe that a
lady who had received a Christian upbringing could appar-
ently be afraid of nothing.

Despite these circumstances, Christ had obtained the
victory. I knew that we were Chinese people and ought to
manage these affairs according to Chinese rules, no matter
how much Miss Zhang Meizhen opposed it. I therefore
went directly to see the Zhang family's legal head of the
house, Mr Zhang Ruiguan, to bring up the marriage subject

with him. He immediately answered, 'The man should marry, the woman should be given in marriage. My niece must promise this, and then there is nothing I cannot do.' He also said, 'We have heard that your son is not in good health. Is this true?' I then very politely told him the true circumstances. He said, 'Although it is so, we cannot but submit to providence.' He promised that when it came to the time of the wedding he would come to Hangzhou to arrange it. Amazingly, because he was to come out and manage the wedding, Miss Zhang Meizhen then staged a big quarrel, making everybody know about it. Oh my God, You are worthy to be praised, because in every kind of trial You alone can lead us through, so I worship before You.

After this affair I felt I ought to have a suitable contact with my future daughter-in-law and see what her spiritual condition really was. I also asked the Lord that if it was His will for her to be my daughter-in-law, He would enable me to love her more than I loved my own daughter. So I requested the Zhang family for leave of absence for her to go with me to Hangzhou so that we could take part together in a special meeting. Thank God, my wish was fulfilled. I slept in one room with her for a week, and we lived together and prayed together. One day at our time of prayer God gave me to see that she really was the one He had prepared to be my son's wife, and I thanked Him.

On the 19th October[16] they were married. This was the day on which my husband and I had been married. After they were married the persecution was more than before. It is true, we are pressed on every side, yet not straightened;

---

[16] 1934.

perplexed, but not despairing; smitten down, yet not destroyed. What the whole of mankind would not dare to do, to say or to write, a group of church members actually dared to do. But I confess I also was defeated, and had not yet, through the sufferings God gave me, come to praise Him. I even said a lot that was not fair. My natural life was very much afraid of the cross. When my gracious Lord's love touched me I was willing with a full heart for the coming of the cross. But when God really answered my request and gave me the cross, my natural form was disclosed, and I began to fear and was not willing to receive it. Moreover, I was still able to evade it. Man's heart truly is unreliable, deceitful above all things, but our wonderful Lord did not, because of my defeat and corruption, cast me off, but on the other hand, because of my weakness, His strength protected me. Although He is Abraham's God and Isaac's God, He himself willingly says He is Jacob's God. How happy we can be about this! Although I can cheat and be crafty like Jacob, the Lord Jesus said His Father is my Father, and His God is my God. Lord Jesus, You are God's Christ; I worship before You.

After this I was invited to go to Beijing. There I stayed in the home of relatives. Because our way was not the same, I endured a lot of attacks and criticism. One day Mrs Wang Mingdao came to see me and asked me to give a little word to the sisters at their meeting place. I felt I should go, and so responded that I would. At the time when Mrs Wang went out she happened to meet my relative coming home, and when he knew Mrs Wang wanted me to go and speak to the sisters he immediately told Mrs Wang that he had invited me to his home to rest because I was physically weak; he certainly had not invited me to come and work. After he had said this, he did not tell me.

When the next day came I prepared to go, and he did not show by his manner the least hindrance, but let me call a conveyance and go. As soon as I got to the meeting place I found the door very firmly shut. I knocked for a while, and then a woman came out and opened the door. When it was time for the meeting I saw that not one person had arrived, so I could not help asking her, 'Is there not a meeting today? Is there a lady from Fuzhou coming here today?' She said there was no meeting and no lady from Fuzhou was coming. It truly made me feel very strange. I further asked whether or not this was Mr Wang Mingdao's meeting place. She said it was. I could only withdraw.

Not long after this, Mrs Wang heard that I had been to the meeting place and was full of shame. She came to the place where I was staying to apologise and told me what my relative had said to her. I then knew I had been deceived, but to the end I did not dare mention it to my relative, but I asked God to open the way for me to stay elsewhere.

While I was waiting quietly, I thought constantly of a fellow student, Mrs Yu Liande, and Miss Huang Shuqiong, and while I was at Tuh Ing girls' school, that very dear Miss Huang's sister. When we were at school, because of her sister, we were very good friends, but after we were married we did not communicate. But she knew how the Lord had been gracious to me and had used me, and I also knew she was not born again and had prayed for her. One day I was talking with my relative about Mrs Yu, and asked him where she then lived. He said he was not willing to tell me, lest I should go and look for her. He also said, 'I tell you honestly, the people she mixes with are all high-class rich ladies like Mrs Zhang Xiaoliang. They dance, meet at feasts and play cards all day long. Miss Pei lives in her home and can't do anything about it. What could you do? She often goes out as a guest, and for the majority of days is not at home.' What my relative saw was my work; what I saw was that God wanted to work, and me to go. Since he was unwilling to tell me Mrs Yu's address, I decided to wait quietly until God's time had come.

After a week, brother Jiang Shoudao invited my husband and me to go together for a meal. We felt we should go, and we replied that we would. When that evening arrived, Mrs Huang Zhengji was also invited to be there. At that time I mentioned my burden for Mrs Yu, and that I wanted to go and bring a flow of the Lord's life to her, etc. When Mrs Huang heard this she was silent. But she was a saved sister and really believed that if God wanted to save her He certainly could save her, moreover He was a God who loved the souls of men. I asked for Mrs Yu's address and she immediately told me it was this road, no. 55. I asked her if she could telephone for me to tell Mrs Yu that I was there and very much wanted to see her. She then got up and went to telephone. In no time she came back with a pleased look and said Mrs Yu asked me to go to her home and meet her at eight o'clock that same evening. I then thanked God with a full heart that He would work.

After the meal we all knelt down and prayed. When we had finished I asked brother Shoudao and his sister to pray continuously. Mrs Huang, my husband and I all three went forth together to the battle. When I came to her home she was very polite and welcomed me exceedingly well. She

took my hand and inquired how I was, and wanted to talk
about other things. I immediately told her that I had come
to see her that day by command upon me. I said, 'It is late.
Allow me to ask whether or not you know your destiny and
where you are going.'

She replied, 'I do not know.'

I then very sincerely and beseechingly said, 'I know my
destiny will be to go to heaven, and moreover I know
where you are going.'

She showed surprise and said, 'How do you know your
and my destinies?'

I then told her, 'The Bible clearly says that believers in the
Lord Jesus will escape perdition and receive eternal life; and
in reverse, unbelievers will surely perish and not obtain
eternal life. What is believing? John 1:12 says, "All who
have received the Lord Jesus" – that is believing. If we only
believe that Jesus exists, Satan also believes, so what use is
it? When people believe in Jesus and receive Him as their
Saviour, at the same time He becomes their life. Man in the
presence of God is a sinner and needs a Saviour; man also
is dead and needs life. If He is your Saviour, you can escape
perdition; if He is your life, you will have eternal life. Moreover, when you have eternal life you will be a child of God;
apart from receiving there is no other way.'

She straight away asked me how we ought to receive. I
said, 'Open the door of your heart, kneel down and receive.
That is all.'

She said, 'May we kneel down together and pray?' So we
knelt down, and when I had finished praying she also
prayed of her own accord, saying, 'Oh Lord, I am a sinner;
I now receive You to be my Saviour and ask You to forgive

my many past sins.' It is very wonderful: as soon as one's heart is opened, the Lord immediately enters, for He is right outside the sinner's heart, knocking at the door, patiently waiting.

Then Mrs Yu had a difficult time, regretting former faults. When the two of us got up, she said, 'I have already received.' Yes, how simple it is for a sinner to receive eternal life, for all other lords are finished by the cross – man only needs to receive. When she got up she embraced me tightly and said much in loving words and thanksgiving to the Lord. I truly saw the Lord's life already in her. I also could not exhaust praise and thanksgiving for the Lord's grace, then we took our leave and returned home.

Three days later, at four o'clock in the afternoon, I had an inward feeling that I ought to go and see Mrs Yu, but I am one who has difficulty in recognising the way, and could only ask God to be merciful and gracious and enable me to find it. Yes, the car driver very easily found her home. When I knocked at the door, Mrs Yu herself was upstairs waiting to know who was there. As soon as she saw it was me, she very joyously invited me upstairs as though there was something special she was waiting for me to come and solve.

When we had sat down she said, 'Oh, sister Heping, the day before yesterday I received the Lord, but I also had another thought come: what is the next step forward? This surely has a sequel. That evening, because I was too excited, I didn't ask your address. I thought of sending somebody to invite you, but I couldn't. Then I remembered you telling me that we may call upon God in all things, and He can undertake for us. So I bowed the knee before the presence of the Lord and said, "Oh God, I previously didn't know this kind of thing, only that when we ask You work for us. Today is the first time I say to You that I want sister Heping to come here; I want to ask her how I go forward in the second step. I ask You to hear my prayer and let me know what manner of God You are – this is my desire." From the time I prayed until now it's only two hours, and indeed you have come. It is true that God can answer prayer. To have God act for me is much quicker than sending somebody to invite you. This is the first experience in my life. God is a living God. I thank Him.'

As she spoke she showed that she was full of gratitude. I told her how God, after I had prayed, had moved me to come. When she heard that the time tallied, her joy was irrepressible. I then told her the truth about believing and being baptised. Naturally what I spoke of was immersion. At first she was a little anxious about her physical condition, and was afraid she could not endure it. At that time it was the middle of July and she was still wearing a long cotton gown. Then I said, 'You should pray to God again, and He will accordingly hear and work for you.' She nodded her head in agreement. By God's leading she was baptised in the name of the Lord Jesus on the 22nd July 1935 at Chu Hsang Hu Jong meeting place.

After this the Lord led me to have several days' talk with the sisters. At first Mrs Yu felt she was physically unable to come every day, but despite that, she came on the first day, and after the meeting, with a heart and mind perfectly satisfied, she said, 'I will come again tomorrow evening.' God is worthy to be praised for His grace to Mrs Yu, enabling her to come from the beginning to the end of the meetings. She also truly saw that she was blessed in body and spirit, and invited all the brethren to a meal at her home. In the joy of that gathering we all felt the presence of the Lord; each one received both in body and in spirit.

After a few days, on the 26th, I was invited to Ten Ching University residence, and I rested there over a month. At this time I heard news from Yantai saying that there were many people there who had received the outpouring of the Holy Spirit and had power to work miracles and such like. I thought I was unworthy and did not need to consider it. But the more I thus decided, the more I felt I must. What the outpouring of the Holy Spirit actually was, I did not know in the least and had never seen.

Again after a little while I decided to return to Shanghai. Mrs Yu entertained me before I left and asked me how I was managing for travelling expenses. I told her that when I came I had enough for the return boat ticket. She said that no matter what, she would certainly give me $200 for pocket money. I firmly refused to accept it and told her she could give it to the church, so she did so. It was good at that time, for the meeting place was too small and they wanted to demolish three rooms to make one large room, and buy chairs and an organ, etc., which needed quite a sum of money.

Mrs Yu said she must give me something as a remembrance. Just as I was leaving she gave me a length of dress material and a fan. I left the fan behind and gave the dress material to a sister to make a new dress when she got married. From this time we did not meet again on earth, for the Lord has already received her to her heavenly home.

As soon as I reached Shanghai and Miss Pei saw me, she

immediately said, 'You should know that Mrs Yu's fervour today is not due to your meritorious service; it is due to my sixteen years' prayer for her.'

I smiled and said, 'Neither is it he that plants anything, nor he that waters, but God that gives the increase. I know that I have no merit, but I also know you have no merit – it is all God Himself who has the merit. If all my work is not condemned, it will be well, but where can one think of merit?'

She said very angrily, 'You needn't think she will behave like you do, because her status is much more honourable than yours.' When I heard this I could only quietly withdraw into God, and I did not utter a word. Before long she got up and went, and I, because of a 'hot summer's day of hard toil', became ill.

At the end of September 1935 Watchman returned to Shanghai with his fellow workers and preached the truth of the outpouring of the Holy Spirit. They had all received the outpouring of the Holy Spirit. What about me? I was just sick in bed at home and heard nothing about it. God is worthy to be praised: on the morning of the 1st October I read Matthew 8:17, 'He himself took our infirmities and bore our diseases.' Then this verse of Scripture shone forth, lighting up my spirit within with unspeakable strength, directly speaking forth the fact to me to cause me to receive it. But – unworthy and stupid me – I read the verse three or four times over, 'He himself took our infirmities and bore our diseases,' yet I was still weakly lying in bed, still carrying my disease there. The Lord has substituted on behalf of, and moreover has borne. And me? I had not obtained what the Lord had accomplished for me. What could I do?

A whole day passed until the evening, as I questioned and answered myself. On the second day, the 2nd October, I awakened and the Lord said to me, 'I am He who took your infirmities and bore your diseases; you can obtain this.'

I then said to the Lord, 'Oh Lord, I cannot believe it; I am not able to believe; I cannot believe; I dare not believe and I don't know how to believe, but I want to believe; I beseech You to give me and make me have faith.' When I saw that in myself I had nothing and could not do anything but call upon Him, He just gave me faith immediately. Very wonderfully, within five or six minutes, my heart was full of faith that He had taken my infirmities and borne my diseases.

When my husband came up to see me, I told him that the Lord Jesus had already taken my infirmities and borne my diseases. He smiled unconcernedly and went downstairs. I, with impressive words, met a husband who heard only vaguely. Truly how difficult this is! I could only shake my head and sigh silently.

At nearly six o'clock in the evening, my eldest daughter-in-law Pinhui came home from school, where she taught, and asked me, 'Mother, are you well today?'

I said, 'The Lord Jesus has taken my infirmities and borne my diseases.' She smiled and went. As to the meaning of this, none of them could make sense of it.

On the third day, the 3rd October, as soon as I awoke the Lord said to me, 'I have already taken your infirmities and borne your diseases. Why don't you get up? Nobody believes this because you don't get up.' So I got up immediately, put on good clothes and stockings and again sat on the bed and took my comb and combed my hair. I had not half done it when I became confused and unconscious, I don't know how long for, but I slowly came to and when I opened my eyes I saw the comb was still in my hand. Thank the Lord, although I went through this, in my heart I still believed that He had taken my infirmities and borne my diseases, because what comes forth from man's faith is lacking – only what comes forth from God's faith is abiding.

So with the utmost strength I finished doing my hair, got off the bed and went downstairs and called the servant to prepare breakfast for me. I ate two slices of bread and drank a cup of milk. By the time I had finished, the servant had already called a conveyance and I went to no. 26 Wen De Li, Hardoon Road, where Miss Li Yuanru (Miss Ruth Lee) lived.

When I entered the room I was filled with the breath of the Spirit, as though my spiritual eyes could see and my spiritual hands could touch. Everybody knelt down to pray and I was the first one to pray, saying, 'Oh Lord, take away my unbelieving, wicked heart. I now want Your Spirit to fill me.' At the same time I stretched out both my hands as though I were receiving a gift. The Lord's Spirit was then greatly poured out on me and my spirit within was greatly filled by the Lord's Spirit. When I arrived I was a weak old lady, but now I was strong and young. I felt as light in body as swansdown, just like a moth coming out of its cocoon ready to fly. Then I truly understood the satisfaction of the words 'He has broken every fetter . . . He has made me free.' I arrived at about eight o'clock and went home at about twelve o'clock.

At this time the Lord helped me to see clearly His calling

me out, that I might entirely regard prayer and preaching as my business, and serve Him. Although I had nine children, they were all grown up and I could put them into the Lord's hands, and I told Watchman this. He said, 'You can have a talk with Miss Li.' So I wrote a letter to Miss Li telling in detail how the Lord had called me out for prayer, preaching and serving Him. Miss Li sent me a reply acknowledging this fact.

One day I was praying for the salvation of all my sons and daughters. I asked God, saying, 'Oh Lord, You said, "Believe on the Lord, and you and your household will all be saved." I have been saved for fifteen years. Why up until now is it not entirely accomplished? Who is hindering You?' My questioning voice had just stopped when the Lord gave me to see that I was the one who was hindering His work. I was very surprised and answered, 'Oh Lord, their father does not take the responsibility of praying for them; even his own salvation is not clear. I have prayed all along for them for fifteen years and have shed many tears for them. Why do You say today that I am hindering Your work? I really do not understand. Please God, tell me plainly.'

This God, merciful to men, is worthy to be praised. He then asked me, 'Can you pray for the souls of others as you pray for your sons and daughters?' I saw immediately that although I prayed for the souls of my sons and daughters, I regarded myself as the centre, and it was to benefit myself, which not only could not please God but also hindered His work. Oh, how fearsome this was. At the same time God gave me to see that as to the salvation of my sons and daughters, although in heart and mouth my thought and voice were to glorify God, really in the depths it was for my own comfort, glory and merit, etc. Jehovah searches the affections and secrets of the heart. Man looks on the outward appearance; God looks on the inside of the heart.

After such an illumination of myself, I submitted before God's presence in confession of sin and asked His forgiveness. My prayer then changed, not regarding myself as the centre, but God as the centre. That year the Lord was gracious to me and some of my sons and daughters were saved. From that time I knew that when praying, although we say it is for God, in the end as a matter of fact it is not necessarily so. God has to dig out the depths before the natural form is revealed. It is possible for us to be deceived, and we can deceive ourselves and even, with delusion, cheat others. If it were not for God's mercy in enlightening us, we really would not know how long we might hinder His work.

Chapter 9

After I received the outpouring of the Lord's Spirit, the testings were greater than before and the hardships were more. These are true facts put before you. The rent of the house in Fuzhou was only enough for my daughter Decheng, who looked after the house, and her daughter Peixin's food and clothing expenses, etc., plus my youngest son Xingzu's school fees, etc. There was no money left over to send to us aged husband and wife. But – proud me – I was unwilling to disclose the lack to others by my manner.

One day I had no alternative but to go to my son's home and borrow $300 to live on. Before long my husband got heart disease, and we had no money to call a doctor. It happened that his second brother and his daughter-in-law came to inquire about the illness, and demanded to know of me what state of mind this was that after over forty years of married life there was no affection prompting me to call a doctor to investigate. If in the end I allowed him to die like this, what about my conscience? They were so angry with me that I did not know what to do for the best, and could only smile and say nothing. This made them more angry, anger which soared to the skies, and they left. After this they did not come again. At home I could only beseech the Lord, and God did not give me any clear sign or supply.

Before long Watchman, without informing us, went to Tianjin, leaving my daughter-in-law daily going out to teach in school. She did not live with us aged ones; we only had the second and fourth sons living together with us, but really when they were out of work and had fallen spiritually, they just ate and drank at home, were dissatisfied outside, and gave me a lot of trouble. For instance, every time they had a bath they were unwilling to let the water out. When I came to have a bath, I first had to let the water out and wash the bath. At first I told them they must let the water out after a bath, but the effect was as though wind passed by their ears; not once did they let the water out.

Once I asked the Lord, 'Oh Lord, now I am old, am I still to go on doing this?'

The Lord answered, 'I came not to be ministered unto, but to minister.' Oh, our wonderful Lord just spoke once and the wind and waves within me were stilled.

After this every day I suffered my two sons' non-affection in life. Not only this, but my husband's illness grew worse every day. One night, at midnight, the Lord awakened me and wanted me to bring to my husband the life of saving grace. At that time my husband also awoke and asked what the matter was. I then preached the Lord's saving grace to him and very directly told him, saying, 'Although you formerly have heard all about the Lord's saving grace, you still have not obtained the Lord's life. Tonight is the time of your salvation. You must not delay any longer. Hurry up and receive.'

Then the Spirit of the Lord worked greatly. He then, before the presence of the Lord who gave His life for us, asked for salvation. Truly that night he clearly was saved by grace.

Although this was so, his illness, as before, became worse each day. On the 20th January 1936 in the morning, when I was praying, I asked the Lord whether my husband would really die. Immediately an inner voice said, 'The grave cannot praise Thee, hell cannot speak of Thy works.' I knew then that God did not want my husband to leave the world now.

When I met Miss Zuo, I asked her to come and pray for my husband, and told her my experience in prayer. She said, 'Although you have a word, if I have no word, what can we do? We had better wait for the Lord's leading.' I did not dare do what I wanted, so when I heard these words I could only go home and see my husband. Inwardly I still had a guarantee because of God's word.

One day passed, and on the second day, the 21st, in the morning, I went again to Miss Zuo to ask for news. She said, 'My original prayer was first of all for myself, but today as soon as I knelt down God wanted me to inquire for Mr Ni Senior. As soon as I besought, God gave me word that I should go and pray for him, so today I will surely go.' I thought she would go with me then, but unexpectedly she wanted to wait until the evening and go together with Miss Gu. I could only get up and go.

That day my husband's illness was exceptionally severe. His heart stopped eleven times, and he fainted away. His feet were cold, he spat saliva and was near death. I truly marvelled that the Lord gave me wonderful faith, that without flurry or hurry I quietly and peacefully waited for the Lord to work and fully believed the Lord would heal him. At that time I took a key and opened a box and took out his winter clothes. When he saw this he turned pale and said, 'What are you taking them out for?' After that day's events, he thought I had got his clothes out because he might die.

But I gave him a transcendent answer, saying, 'This evening Miss Zuo and others are coming to pray for you. God said He will heal you, and He wants you to get up this evening. That is why I've got your clothes out, lest you should not be ready then, with nothing you can wear, because from the end of September 1935 right up to now, over four months, you have been in bed.'

When he heard this he was pleased and smiled, and fainted again. This time he was unconscious much longer than before, but the Lord's grace was more manifest than before. Not only did I not doubt God, but I opened my mouth in song and praise, waiting for the evening for God to work on his body. Before long he came to again.

In the evening Miss Zuo and Miss Gu came together to my home. My eldest daughter-in-law, Pinhui, also came – four people with one heart and mind to pray for God's glory. Miss Zuo was the first to pray, and I followed. When I prayed to the point of touching God's power, the Holy Spirit was mightily poured forth and I spoke in a tongue, praising God's glory. While I was praising God, my husband got up of his own accord, put on his socks and clothes, and also knelt beside the bed and sang, 'Hallelujah, glory to the Lord! Hallelujah! Amen. Hallelujah, glory to the Lord who raised me up again.' We saw that he was already healed and greatly praised God and the Lamb who was slain, our Lord Jesus Christ, right up until ten o'clock. We stopped because we were afraid of disturbing our neighbours. Otherwise we would have praised until dawn.

The next day my husband got up early, and himself got the basin and hot water and washed his face. In every way that I had formerly served him he did not want me to do so again. He could do it all himself.

After two days Satan began to do a swindling work and said to my husband, 'You are not healed; it was just all in your mind.' Thank God, my husband not only did not believe the devil's word, but could declare to him, saying, 'I believe I am healed.' One day his heart trouble rose up again, and he laughed sarcastically at Satan, saying, 'Satan, you are really stupid. Why must you be like this? No matter what, I know that I am healed. Satan, be off!' From that time he lived another five years, and was unusually strong until the 18th December 1941, when he was called to heaven.

I remember that while my husband was sick I read the scripture which says, 'Rejoice in the Lord always, and again I say rejoice' (Philippians 4:4). The Holy Spirit wrought this in my life, causing me to rejoice. I then asked Him, 'Oh Lord, I have no way of rejoicing. My husband is sick in bed, I have no money for doctor or medicine, my two sons are at home out of work, what comes in from the rent in Fuzhou is less than expenditure. How can I rejoice?' But when I bowed before the Lord, the Holy Spirit was mightily poured out and my heart was incomparably glad, and I sang, 'I have the Lord and rejoice. . .'[17]

---

[17] The whole hymn is given in the original.

By this I saw that if man's happiness is because his environment is prosperous and his wealth abundant, that happiness is not lasting. When the eye is turned round it is seen not only not to give happiness, but to be grievous. I truly know that whatever man loves in this world, that is the most injurious thing in his life. No matter if it is husband, wife, children, riches, friends, gaming or wealth – if your heart is gripped by these they have power to dismiss you to the place of death. If you do not believe it, you will experience it yourself one day. I profoundly know that our God is one who hates evil, and if we have anything outside Him for which we have an ardent desire, it will become a source of creating wounds. I truly thank God that from that day He gave me to receive the Lord's joy. Although very much sorrow and grief of heart have come upon me, and although I have passed through the valley of weeping, before long I again received the Lord's joy. I record here now an ever-unalterable judgement that if you have the Lord, you have joy; if you have not the Lord, you have not joy.

My second daughter, Guizhen, got an internal disease. Although she went through much surgery and spent a lot of money, the disease was just the same. She saw how well I was and that her father's illness had been cured by the Lord, and she had an ardent desire in her heart. But she dared not speak, because formerly she had disliked me very much, and was afraid I would talk doctrine to her. She did not in the least agree with what I believed and did. I remember once she brought a subscription book asking us to subscribe towards building a church. At that time I had already received light and saw how our money should be solely for God's use, not spent on good works and human feelings, so I did not subscribe. She blamed me much. Besides, God also enlightened me not to receive presents from my sons and daughters at the annual festivals, because all the festivals had Satan's work and meaning in them, so I announced to them not to give again. Exodus 23:24 says, 'You shall not worship their gods, nor serve them, and shall not do according to their ways.' Giving presents at festivals is pagan; I serve God, so I refuse to receive. But this inevitably began to cause much misunderstanding, hurting feelings in the process. Nonetheless, God is worthy to be praised. He Himself has become my rest.

I also decided not to receive birthday gifts from my sons and daughters. I felt that surely nobody kept my Lord's birthday for him when he was on the earth. The servant cannot be above his master; the student cannot be above his teacher. So on another occasion I had an argument with my sons and daughters – it was on my fiftieth birthday. Four of them were married. The fourth daughter had just been married, and she did not in the least understand my heart and my way of life, so before my birthday she and her husband came from Xiamen to Fuzhou to offer birthday congratulations. The sons and daughters who were already there were all waiting to see how I would treat this newly married daughter and son-in-law. In this instance I was nearly defeated, because I felt they had come on a long journey, travelling over land and sea, and if I altogether refused it would inevitably cause a great distancing of our close relationship. To compromise with them would mean a lack of peace in my heart.

When they wanted me to agree to celebrate, I withdrew, saying, 'Wait until I have asked God,' but really, because of their sincere thought, I was already wavering. That evening I prayed about this matter and in my spirit felt as though God did not want to hear this hypocritical prayer. No matter what, in my heart I still cherished the fear of God. So in the middle of the night I got up and inquired before God, saying, 'Oh God, speak to me.'

I remembered my former life of partying and sin, and felt God then said, 'How crafty you are: you daily ask Me for the deeper death of the old Adam, but today you inwardly have a desire to receive people who have set their mind on birthday congratulations. What kind of inconsistency is this?'

I immediately got up and confessed my sin, knowing myself to be an unreliable person. If God had not protected me from this vanity, I do not know to what place I soon would have fallen. Today the fact that I can write here of this work upon me is all due to God's care and protection. May glory be to Him. Amen.

The next morning my sons and daughters begged for an answer, and I replied saying, 'No.'

They said, 'You need not be involved in arranging the feast and inviting guests, and you need not spend the money. It will be all right if you just agree.'

I said, 'I dare not agree, because I dare not sin against God. If you definitely want to do it, I will immediately leave home and go away.'

They saw that I was steadfastly steeled against it, disappointing their hopes, and could not help expressing their dissatisfaction to me. It seemed they were more concerned with their own desires and wishes than with mine! After this, sadly mother and daughter had no love between them in life.

When the day came that the doctor could do no more for Guizhen, it was well that I went to her home that day. She told me how she had poured out her heart to the Lord, and hoped the Lord would be merciful and heal her. I said, 'I will go and tell Miss Zuo. If God says He will heal you, I will come again and tell you.' While Miss Zuo and I were praying together, we felt that God would heal her. I then took her to where Miss Zuo lived, and it was fortunate that brother Li was there also, so we commenced to pray together. The Holy Spirit at that time was greatly poured out on her and she then obtained life and healing. I also told her the truth that a woman's long hair is her glory, but short hair is a shame, and the truth of head-covering. It was very wonderful that when the grace of God worked, there was nothing she did not understand and receive. When it came to the sisters' meeting on Saturday afternoon, she stood up and gave her testimony, speaking Fuzhou dialect, and I interpreted into Mandarin for her. Two weeks later she could testify in Mandarin. The Lord's grace was upon her, causing her spiritual life to advance and grow. God is worthy to be praised. I want to be one who sings, 'Although love is difficult to return, and grace difficult to repay, I only wish to praise well.'

During this period I often went with Miss Zuo to visit the sisters in their homes, pray and heal diseases, etc. Before long Miss Zuo went to Hangzhou to work, and I stayed in Shanghai. One day Miss Gu came by taxi to where I lived, saying, 'There is a Mrs Kueh who has come back from France, and she has a four-year-old daughter, suffering from epilepsy, in Hong Ngen Hospital. The doctor has already pronounced that there is no hope, so she thought if only you could go and pray for her, then the child will be healed. Please will you go now?'

I answered, 'The gracious gift of healing is one God has given to Miss Zuo. I do not have this gift of grace. It would be better to wait until Miss Zuo comes back.'

Just then the Lord inwardly said to me, 'You also have this gift of grace. I have already given it to you. You go.'

At this time I was really fearful and confused, and asked myself, 'If prayer does not heal, what will you do?' So I again said to the Lord, 'Oh Lord, I dare not go. I'm afraid I won't pray well.'

The Lord said, 'Go. I am with you and will heal her.'

I had no alternative but to go with Miss Gu. But although we were going, in my heart I wished the taxi would go a little slower. When we reached the door of Hong Ngen Hospital I said to the Lord, 'May You glorify Your own name.' Then my heart fully knew that the Lord would heal her.

We entered the sickroom and the mother, who was lying down beside the child, immediately got up and told me the symptoms of the disease. We then knelt down, and while we were praying the Holy Spirit was greatly poured upon me. As soon as I placed my hands on the child, rebuked the disease, and in the name of Jesus commanded it to depart, the child's pain immediately obeyed and left her.

Mrs Kueh said, 'As soon as you entered the door I knew the child would certainly be healed.' She invited me to go again the next day. I replied that when I had time I would surely go, and I wanted to preach the gospel to her. On the third day I went to the hospital again and saw the child already sitting up by herself on the bed, playing as though she had not been sick. I preached the gospel to Mrs Kueh and thanked the Lord for them. After this Miss Gu and I went home together.

On the way back Miss Gu wanted me to go and pray for Miss Chen and heal her. She had been ill for five days; her eyes could not bear the light, and black curtains were drawn over the window and door. Miss Li Yuanru (Ruth Lee) had also told Miss Gu to ask me to pray for her and ask the Lord to heal her. I answered, 'I am extremely exhausted, but in my spirit I am not tired. I will go with you.' Naturally I dared not say no, and the car proceeded to Miss Chen.

We sang and prayed and the Lord gave us a word from 2 Corinthians 1:20: 'For however many be the promises of God, in Christ they are all "yes", wherefore also through him they are all true, unto the glory of God through us.' We prayed to this point, and Miss Chen was then healed and got up straight away. We praised God, and at the same time we helped Miss Chen to dress. We returned home after ten o'clock, not only not tired, but with heavenly joy, glory and strength. Psalm 126:6 says, 'He that goes on his way weeping, bearing forth the seed, he shall come again with joy, bringing his sheaves with him.' The word of the Lord is steadfast, so I say God is worthy to be praised unto eternity. Amen.

Chapter 10

After this I went out a great deal, praying and healing. Before long Watchman and Miss Li jointly sent a telegram to Shanghai asking me to go to Shantou to work. After I received the telegram I could not decide for myself. I could only place it before the church prayer meeting, full of hope that the church's reply would be that I should not go to Shantou, because at this time I was very reluctant to leave the spiritual atmosphere and work in the Shanghai church. Yet God spoke in the prayer meeting, and everybody thought I should go. So I sent a telegram to the Shantou church to ask if my husband and I could go. The reply telegram said we could. So we went together and by God's grace had a peaceful journey and arrived at Shantou. This was the first time I did not experience seasickness. I truly thank God, who treated this chief of sinners graciously.

On my arrival at Shantou God gave me to see that of myself I could do nothing. First there was three weeks' work, daily prayer in the mornings and in the afternoons, according to the Lord's leading, visiting the sisters. After three weeks there was a daily morning prayer meeting as before, right up until the time I left Shantou. In the evenings there was the sisters' training meeting. Before long a reading class was added for sisters who could not read, teaching them to read, learn Scripture verses and sing choruses, etc. Later we saw many sisters coming out to witness for the Lord and preach the gospel. We truly saw the Lord's blessing and mercy.

After some time I knew the Lord wanted me to leave Shantou and go to Hong Kong. If it had not been for God's grace, I would again have come down to being unwilling to leave Shantou. In this I saw I was one specially protected, for according to my original nature, being gripped by the work, I do not know to what place I would have fallen. God is faithful and to be trusted for ever. Amen.

After I arrived in Hong Kong there were special meetings, and for several days I witnessed for the Lord. After the meetings I went to Canton and saw brother Jiang Shoudao (Stephen Kaung). In Canton the Lord also had a little work, and He healed the body of Mrs Andrew Lin and her spirit received new life. Before many days letters kept coming from all round Shantou asking me to return, and they even sent two brothers to take me back. But the Lord had not given the word and I dared not move. He is greatly to be feared. Before long I returned to Hong Kong with brother Stephen Kaung. At that time my husband also went to Hong Kong and lived with me, and there I worked together with brothers Wei Guangxi and Lu Zhongxing (Faithful Luke). Afterwards the Lord again led me to Macao, Taishan, Chongshan and such places to proclaim His name.

The son of Mr Qiang Qunji of Long Li Company in Hong Kong knew that God had given me the gift of healing. One

Friday he wrote a letter to me saying that he had more than ten strange lumps on his body and he desired God to heal him. When I put the letter before God, He very wonderfully answered me, saying, 'You go. Both the father and son will be healed.' I did not understand why God said both father and son, because only the son had asked for healing, but I believed the facts laid before me, and could only quietly wait for God. When Sunday morning came, God made the matter clear. That morning Mrs Qiang Qunji came and told me that on Saturday evening her husband had spat a lot of blood, and asked me to go immediately to heal him. So I responded.

That day, when the afternoon meeting was over, at about six o'clock, I went to the Qiang home and first preached the saving grace of the Lord Jesus to Mr Qiang. He immediately saw his sin and simultaneously received the Lord Jesus to be his Saviour, and at the same time I prayed for his illness and he was healed. There was a doctor there who said prayer was prayer, but on the other hand it was still necessary to give injections and medicines. I then said to this doctor, 'If you give injections and medicines, you must take responsibility for the life of this patient. Otherwise God will take responsibility, because God said He would heal both father and son.' So he dared not give an injection.

On Tuesday morning I returned to the home. Mr Qiang Qunji was already able to get up and had the noon meal with us, and nobody could exhaust their thanks to the Lord. After another week he was managing his business as before. Before long he was baptised in the name of the Lord. Up until the time of writing, this disease has not recurred.

As to his son's strange lumps on his body, on the day that

his father was healed I also laid hands on him and prayed, but he was not healed that day. After a few days, when he was washing, he knew he was already healed. *When* he was healed, even he himself did not know. Oh my God, You are faithful; Your word is settled in the heavens and for ever more, and I therefore worship before You.

One day my son invited me to go with him to Macao to rest a while and enjoy the scenery of the place. I turned inward and knew the Lord was not permitting me to go. My husband also asked me, saying, 'Aren't you going?' I answered that I could not, and he was very unhappy and urged me strongly to go. I could only shut my mouth and not speak. After a while my eldest daughter-in-law, Pinhui, came to set the luggage in order for us, wanting us to go together to Macao. I then very determinedly said to her, 'Charity, I am not going to be influenced by you today. I am definitely not going, because the Lord does not permit me.' She had first thought to make me go, but she also feared God and, hearing me speak like this, dared not be obstinate. They all went, leaving me alone at home.

That evening I went to bed particularly early. There were two sisters living with us. At two o'clock in the night somebody knocked at the door very urgently. When I opened the door I saw Mrs Zhao Xiwei, who had come to ask me to pray for her husband. She said he was very ill and life could be gone in an instant. Could she ask me to go and pray for him now? Hateful me – I answered, 'We will speak again tomorrow. You go back.'

In an instant I felt a lack of peace in my heart and immediately asked the Lord, 'Lord, do You want me to go?'

The Lord said, 'I do.'

I said again, 'Shall I go now or wait until tomorrow?'
The Lord said, 'Go now.'

I dared not disobey the command. I immediately went to ask Miss Lin, who lived with me, to go also. Mrs Ceng also got up and prepared tea and so on for us. When we had finished washing and dressing, we went. When we were halfway there, the Lord said to me, 'This man loves wickedness more than he loves his own soul. You must go quickly and preach the gospel to him.'

So when I got to his home, I first preached the gospel to him. The Lord truly was gracious to him and gave him a sorrowful and bitterly repentant spirit. He took his wife's hand and said, 'I have sinned against you. Please forgive me.' From the time that he had taken a concubine he had treated his wife harshly. Not only so, but because his wife often came to me where I lived, he thought she had been deceived by me. When I previously heard that he was not willing for his wife to visit me, a voice within my spirit said that one day even he himself would need me. Truly, it was because of his own need that his wife asked me to pray for him that night. Thank God, He truly is a merciful God. Mr Zhao not only saw himself as a sinner and received the Lord Jesus to be his Saviour, but he also asked me to lay hands on him and pray that he might be healed. Thanks to God's grace, his body was also healed. On the third day he went to his office. Before long he was also baptised and belonged to the name of the Lord.

There was a Dr Pan Zuoqin who came from Shantou to Hong Kong, who had left to study in England for twelve years and was a most sincere gentleman. On one occasion in the interior of China he met with local bandits and was terrified. Because the shock was so deep, his nerves were disordered. He could not speak and did not sleep or eat. It needed somebody to force him, then he ate, and to force him to sleep, then he slept, but he would not speak. His wife is our brother Chow Tao K'ang's sister. (Robert Chow is a responsible brother now in Singapore.) Because of brother Chow's introduction, his wife came to see me. At first I did not dare make a move. Then one day I knew God's will and went to see him. As soon as he saw me, he showed that he was very fearful. (Afterwards he said that when he saw me a voice said to him that this person was able to harm him.) At this time not only were his nerves bad, but he was possessed by an evil spirit.

Trusting the power of the risen Lord, I asked him, 'Do you know me?' At first he took no notice of my question, then I said to him powerfully, 'You should answer.'

He then nodded and said, 'I recognise you.'

I ordered him to sit up, and he sat up. First I preached the gospel to him, then I ordered him to kneel down and pray together with me. I also told him that when I had prayed a sentence, he should say 'Amen'. By the Lord's great power, he obeyed completely. When we had finished praying, I got up and he still knelt there waiting. I told him to get up and he then dared to get up. That day was Tuesday. As to healing, I had as yet no assurance.

Early on Sunday morning my spirit within was greatly troubled. I did not know what big thing had happened, and went up to the roof of the house to pray. I could not at that time touch the centre of prayer until I mentioned the name of Pan Zuoqin, then inwardly I sensed I had got through. That was the first time the Lord had used His power through me to pray and heal in a way that was not limited by space. I prayed in one place, and he in another place was healed on that day at that time. I thank God that what He does is right, lest I should get glory because of my work, and myself suffer loss. In a few days Dr Pan was baptised in the name of the Lord, and is now a responsible brother in the Hong Kong church.

Before long there was also a lady named Mrs Lu, from Shantou, who had suffered from tuberculosis for more than three years. She was sent away from a hospital managed by French people because they recognised that she was incurable. Her daughter knew that the Lord had given me the gift of healing and came to ask me to lay hands on her and pray. But inwardly I did not have the Lord's leading and dared not respond. She then thought I was a superior person holding back for a better price, so said a whole lot which was unpleasant and which she should not have said. But the Lord allowed this matter to fall on me so that I would learn patience and humility and not be distressed about it.

As much as three months later, suddenly one Wednesday the Spirit of the Lord moved me to go and pray for Mrs Lu and heal her disease. I said, 'Oh Lord, I dare not go, for her disease is already critical. I myself don't believe that she can get well. If this moving is from You, please move me again tomorrow.'

The next day the Lord clearly told me again to go and pray for her, that she might be healed. I said again, 'Oh Lord, I really cannot believe. Please give me faith and move me again tomorrow with full faith.'

On the third day I certainly fully believed that the Lord would make this tubercular woman get up and glorify God's own name. So I went with great courage and prayed for her, and in the name of the Lord commanded this woman who was near to death to get up. She then immediately got up and could walk by herself, do her hair, wash her face and change her clothes. She felt hungry and ate a big meal.

The next day she came by taxi to my home and wanted me to go with her to the meeting. When the meeting was over she suddenly turned dizzy; her face was the colour of death, her lips white, her hands and feet icy cold, and she almost died. Many people thought she would die, but God was merciful to us. God gave me to know that she was like this because she was hungry. So I gave her milk to drink. When she had finished it she immediately opened her eyes and said she would go back with us by taxi. After this, she took nourishment seven times a day, and before long her body was strong and she could walk to the meetings. Oh our God, You truly are a God who raises from the dead. May glory and praise be given to You for ever. Amen.

On the 22nd November 1937, at three o'clock in the night, the Lord called me to get up and worship Him. When this voice came my whole body had no strength, like one about to die. But inwardly I very clearly knew it was the Lord speaking to me, so I answered, saying, 'Oh Lord, I cannot get up, for I have no strength.'

He then said to me, 'I will give you strength.'

So strength gradually came to me and before long I could get up, and when I had dressed, combed and washed it was already five o'clock. I then went into a small room, knelt down and bowed in prayer. Then the Lord asked me, saying, 'Do you know the price of worship?'

I answered, 'Oh Lord, I do not know.'

He said, 'Satan knows. You look at Matthew 4:8–9.'

I immediately opened the Bible and found it, and it said, 'The devil again took Him up into a high mountain and showed Him all the kingdoms of the world and the glory of them and said to Him, "All these will I give You if You will bow down and worship me."' From this I could see that one act of worship from Satan's viewpoint was more important and valuable than all the kingdoms and all the glory of them. He would part with all the kingdoms and their glory to obtain the worship of the Son of God. How great a price was this? I felt I then knew a little of the price of worship to God.

The Lord also asked me, 'How ought you to worship God?' I delayed and could not answer. He then led me to John 4:22–23, 'The time is coming and now is that true worshippers of the Father must worship Him in Spirit and truth, for the Father seeks such to worship Him. God is a Spirit, so they that worship Him must worship in Spirit and in truth.' At the same time He also gave me to see that our Lord did not tell the matter of worship to anybody, but only to the woman of Samaria. It is true that where sin abounded, grace did much more abound, and I worship Him.

The Lord then asked me, 'In the endless ages, do you know what you will do?' All the more I did not know how to answer, but the Lord who is worthy to receive men's worship also gave me to see Revelation 15:2–5.

From that time I tasted a little savour of worship, and I began to study the worship of God and to preach the truth of worship. The Lord also gave me Revelation 14:6–7. That day the Lord showed me that other gospels will pass away;

only the gospel of worship will remain for ever. My former work, only causing people to repent and be saved and healed, was not the best, although the Lord got a little glory. I had not yet attained to God's need in man. So I was willing to drop all my work and only be a worshipper of God.

In one of Kai Nengfu's books on simple prayer he says, 'Nearness to God embraces all service.' Here today I also say that to worship God is the highest service and the attaining of the object of God's salvation. Prayer to God and drawing near to God is man receiving something from God; worship of God is God receiving something from man. Every Christian not only receives God, but ought to allow God to receive something from us. Today Satan is truly wicked; he lets God's children pray but not worship. In the Old Testament times it was also like this, so God through his servant David said, 'All the ends of the earth shall remember and turn unto the Lord, and all the kindreds of the nations shall worship before You' (Psalm 22:27). He also said, 'Give unto the Lord, O ye sons of the Mighty, give unto the Lord glory and strength. Give unto the Lord the glory due unto His name, worship the Lord in the beauty of holiness' (Psalm 29:1–2).

After some days God led me, together with my eldest daughter-in-law, to go to Yunnan Province. The Lord wanted me to work a little in Kunming. On the evening of the second day there, there was a brother who had just believed in the Lord. He had a very good position in aviation, but because of a fall from the plane had gone to hospital for healing. He came to see me, and when we met he was overcome with joy. After we had parted I was surprised that he had not asked me to pray for him and seek healing, for inwardly I knew that he ought to be healed, because the Lord wanted him to be healed.

Sure enough, the next morning he came and said to me, 'Mother, yesterday evening I did wrong because I did not ask you to pray for me that I might be healed. After I got home I was very distressed inwardly and couldn't be more sorry – that is why I have come this morning.'

I listened until he had finished speaking, smiled, and then quickly combed and washed and prepared everything properly, then prayed for him. Thank God, he immediately loosened the splint on his foot and gave it to me. He went home happily, thanking God's grace all the way. After this he often came to see me. He could write very well, and wrote for me Philippians 3:10, 'That I might know Christ, and the power of His resurrection, and the fellowship of His sufferings, like unto His death.' Two years ago his aeroplane had a misfortune and he is now asleep in the Lord.

The responsible brethren in Yunnan definitely wanted me to minister to the sisters for about ten days, and God also gave me an inward burden to witness for the Lord. When I testified as to how the Lord had healed my own sickness and had used me for the healing of many others, there was a Dr Ni who heard but did not believe and disagreed. He said this was entirely psychological and it was necessary for people's organs of sense to be healed before he was willing to believe. Truly God vindicates Himself by works and shows that He is God and is able to do that which the world cannot believe.

One day there was an elderly lady, about fifty years old, who had been deaf for twenty-five years. She came and asked me to pray for her, and God was gracious to her and she was healed. One day after the meeting somebody spoke to her in a loud voice. She smiled and told the person not to speak in such a loud voice again, because her ears were healed. Although it was so, there were still many who doubted and did not believe.

A few days later, while I was preaching, a girl of about eighteen named Wang Xiuzhen stood in the hall making an unceasing disturbance and misbehaving. At first I thought she was possessed by a demon. After the meeting we learned that when she was three years old she had been very ill, and had been given the wrong medicine, which had made her deaf and dumb. They then brought this girl to my home, and I could only ask God what to do about her. Praise God, He is worthy to be praised. Come and glorify God Himself, who would heal this girl.

Together with my daughter-in-law Pinhui, Mrs Yin Zulan and several other sisters, we knelt down and with one heart and mind prayed for God's glory. God showed me that I needed to put two fingers into the hollows of her ears. She immediately received the strength of healing and cried out loudly, but she could not speak words. God again told me to put my finger into her mouth and order her to say, 'Christ is victorious.' She immediately obeyed the command and, following me slowly word by word, said, 'Christ is victorious.' I also said, 'Praise the Lord,' and she said the same. Because we had all seen the Lord make the deaf hear and the dumb speak, we gave glory to our Father and our God. The next day we all went up the West Mountain. This girl who had received grace also went along with us and we saw that she was unusually happy.

After this there was a Mrs Lo, aged sixty-five, who had

been gripped by the opium demon for forty years. When she was twenty-five she began to take opium because of illness. The year she was sixty-five, sister Chen Huixiang preached the gospel to her and she was saved, but she still had no way of breaking off the opium habit and her sickness was not healed. One day I preached the truth of death with Christ and baptism to her and she was altogether moved and willing to obey, so she came to the place where I was staying and asked us to pray for her. Brother Yin and his wife, myself and my daughter-in-law, altogether four people, in the name of the Lord commanded the opium devil to leave, and the devil obeyed us.

On the third day her old disease came back, so her daughter, Mrs Zhang, also a sister, at nine o'clock at night sent somebody to ask us to go quickly and pray for healing, for they feared that delay would endanger her life. After we heard this news we felt the Lord wanted us to go and pray for her. When we had reached her home and prayed silently, we sang hymn no. 154, and before we had finished singing God's strength came upon her and she was healed. In the name of the Lord we commanded the disease to leave her, and forbade it to return. Truly, it did not return.

For many years she had not eaten rice, only eggs and a few tonics and things easily digested. She did not dare to eat the least thing besides. From this time she began to eat half a bowl of rice at each meal. By the time I left Kunming, she was eating two bowls of rice at each meal. While I was there, there was a special meeting and she walked both there and back again. The Lord was gracious to her and she was baptised in the name of the Lord.

The first time she stood up to give her testimony to the

Lord, she really did not understand anything. She partly prayed and partly testified and said what she had received from God. Some people laughed at her, but she did not mind in the least. The second time she stood up to testify, she had made much progress on the first time. The third time it truly moved my heart and glorified the name of the Lord. Our merciful God greatly used her in Dali, Yunnan, to lead many people to belong to the name of the Lord. Hallelujah, Christ is victorious unto extremity. Amen.

In Yunnan there was a lot of work besides; I cannot relate it all here. One day a telegram came from Shantou wanting me to go and work there. I placed this telegram before God. In the evening, during the meeting, God's word came: 'Go towards the south.' So I did not worry about the work, but immediately prepared to go. Although the brothers and sisters were unwilling to let me go, because it was God's command nobody dared say anything.

On the morning that I was to leave, there was a heavy downpour of rain. All along the way the water rose so that it was barely passable. At that time brother Yin said to me, 'Mother, perhaps God doesn't want you to go today. Could we not ask to alter the time?'

I answered, 'Let us pray and see how the Lord leads.' He prayed first, and afterwards I prayed, saying, 'God, if You want me to go today, when I command the rain to stop in the name of Your Son, I pray You will make it stop.'

When I had prayed in this way, a child in the Yin home called out loudly, 'The rain has already stopped and the sun has come out.' This truly made people unable to say that our God does not dwell among us. Under these circumstances, I did not pray again as to whether it was His will or not for me to go; I only asked that all the way I would be led and ordered according to His will and peaceful arranging.

This time on the boat the wind and rain were very heavy, and I was very seasick. But there was a special experience in that there were fifty-four water buffaloes all round the hold of the ship. At first the foul odour of the buffaloes made me severely sick, and it was very difficult. Afterwards I suddenly thought that our Lord slept in an ox manger when He came to this earth. In heaven He was glorious, holy and honourable. Even if He had been born in a royal palace on earth it would have been lowly – how much more lowly to come down and be born in an ox stable. Oh, I am but a low, unbearable person: why shouldn't I today, because of the Lord, dwell with buffaloes? What is the difficulty? When I thought like this, it turned the foul odour of the buffaloes into a sweet aroma and joy for me. I travelled in peace all the way to Hong Kong.

The local responsible brothers and sisters asked me, together with sisters Yu Sucheng and Li Leqi (Rachael Li), to preach the gospel for ten days. After a time of prayer, we responded that we would do this. That night sister Yu Sucheng suddenly became ill. Sister Rachael Li naturally took the responsibility of looking after her. Although I was extremely weak from seasickness, almost unable to respond to the call, God's grace on this old weak body was all the more perfectly manifested. On Monday, the first day, as I was preaching I really felt greatly strengthened in body, and not a few people were saved. When the preaching was over, both body and spirit felt much better than before.

That evening Mrs Qiang Qunji brought Mrs Xiying along.

She said, 'Mr Li Xiying has got something on his thigh which is extremely painful; he has consulted many doctors and they have no way of healing him. I told her that my husband and son were both healed by the Lord, and there is nothing that can be done for Mr Li's disease except to ask the Lord to send His handmaiden Mother Ni from Yunnan back to Hong Kong to pray for him that he may be healed. So the two of us, day and night, have besought and prayed in the presence of God, and it is true, He has sent you. Tonight we have not only come to hear the gospel, we have also come to invite you to visit Mr Li's home and lay hands on him and pray for him.'

I said, 'Let me ask the Lord, and I will answer you tomorrow.'

The next morning I prayed about this matter. The Lord said to me, 'He has asked you. Give to him!'

On Tuesday evening I continued preaching the gospel. After the meeting those two came and asked for news, and I answered them according to the word of the Lord. I agreed to go to Mr Li's home on Wednesday morning at ten o'clock to lay hands on him and pray for him.

The next day I went together with my eldest daughter-in-law, and we preached the gospel to the people in the home. Thank the Lord, the whole family was saved and baptised in the name of the Lord. Mr Li's illness naturally began to be healed. That evening he was able to go to the meeting and hear the gospel. After this he came every evening.

After three weeks Mrs Li came and told me that the lump on her husband's thigh was originally as big as a cucumber, but was now as small as a green pear – yet daily there was a flow of blood and water. Could they not ask me to go again and pray for him, so that he could be completely healed? So I asked the Lord inwardly, and He reminded me that when He was in the world and healed that blind man, at first he only saw men like trees; when the Lord touched him again, then he saw everything clearly. This being so, the next day I went to the Li home as before, together with my daughter-in-law, to lay hands on him and pray for him. From this time he was healed. Now this husband and wife bear some little responsibility in interpreting for workers who come from other places to minister. This truly helps us to see God's grace and salvation.

Chapter 11

Before long Miss Ruth Li, together with several fellow workers, came to Hong Kong and stayed with us some days, then returned to Shanghai, leaving Miss Peace Wang with us. Several months later she also went to South-east Asia. Then a telegram came from the Shanghai church asking me, together with brothers Hua Xipin and Zhen Zexin, to attend special meetings. When we arrived at Shanghai we lived in my eldest son's home, fully expecting to sell the house in Fujian and get a good sum of money, so that my husband and I could live better in our old age.

In the summer of 1940, because my blood pressure was too high and fearing I could not bear the heat of summer, my son sent a special telegram to brother Zhang Xiji at Qingdao to ask him to look for a house for us. Thank God, he provided two rooms for us, and sister Jiang Shuqing lived with us. Before long brother Ding Chengfang asked me to go to Weixian for several days, and also to Qilu University for a week, then back to Qingdao for a fortnight, and back to Shanghai to stay, as before, in my son's home.

At the beginning of December 1941, I received a telegram from Hong Kong asking the Shanghai church to pray about my husband's dangerous illness. The next day Guizhen returned home with the news. It was good that Miss Zuo also came to my home, and the three of us knelt down to pray. At first, following our human feelings, we asked the Lord to heal him, and asked the Lord to let me go to Hong Kong and look after him. But when I touched Him who is God, I immediately changed my prayer, saying, 'Oh Lord, You are God. If it is Your will that I should fall short in my duty to my husband, I say "Amen".'

When I had prayed to this point, I knew inwardly that this time my husband would certainly leave this world, but I did not know whether it would be sooner or later, so I made all the preparations and waited for a boat to the south. Unexpectedly, on the 8th December (with the outbreak of the Japanese–Allies war and Japanese occupation of Shanghai) there was a sudden emergency and communications between Hong Kong and Shanghai were broken off.

In the midst of these circumstances my spirit was in an unceasing battle, and I did not know what to do for the best. We had been married for forty years and I truly felt it hard that at the end we could not see each other. I also thought how very bad I myself had been. Although my sons and daughters had all fulfilled their requirements of filial piety, I had never tasted love between mother and sons and mother and daughters. I had been unfilial to my mother, and had not treated my sons and daughters well. Now God was judging me, how ought I to receive it? How could I dare not submit to it?

Oh my God, You are God, You are worthy to receive my praise and worship. At that time, in those circumstances, I felt darkness all around with no way for my feet, and with words to say but nobody to whom I could express them. I could only cry to the Lord. I knew that only He was willing to be compassionate to this chief of sinners. I asked God to show clearly the way I ought to go, whether I ought to live in my eldest son's home in my old age and serve God, or whether I ought to go out preaching again and serve Him.

In my heart I secretly chose to go out and preach and work for the Lord. But on the first day the Lord gave me to see that Christ's victory on the cross was perfectly completed, and even God Himself had no need to add anything, so how much more useless it was for me to do anything.

On the second day the Lord gave me to see three different things about the cross. The cross of the Lord Jesus Christ was the Sinless One substituting the sinner and receiving the punishment; the One who ought not to die being willing to die for those who ought to die. The Lord asked me to choose from the two following things about the cross:

(1) The condemned prisoner derided the Lord Jesus, saying, 'If You are Christ, how is it You cannot save Yourself, and us?' He was a sinner unwilling to bear the punishment of judgement, and in an attitude of ridicule sought to be saved from it. The Lord Jesus is Christ, and He did not save Himself or him.

(2) Another was the other condemned prisoner, who heard what that man said and answered him with reproof,

saying, 'Since you are receiving the same punishment, don't you fear God? Our punishment is due because what we receive is fitting with what we have done, but this man has not done anything bad.' He then said to the Lord, 'Oh Jesus, when You come into Your kingdom, please remember me.' Jesus said to him, 'I tell you truly, today you will be with Me in paradise.'

They were both condemned prisoners, they were both crucified beside the Lord; there was not the least difference, but their inward view was different. One thought he ought not to be crucified and sought deliverance, and the other saw that crucifixion was due and that the punishment he received was fitting with what he had done previously. But he testified that the Lord Jesus was crucified without sin, and he knew that He was a king who would surely come again. He did not ask to be saved from the cross now; he only asked the Lord to remember him when He came into His kingdom, because he recognised himself and the Lord Jesus and was not in the least confused. The destiny of the two prisoners was entirely different; one went down to Hades lamenting, and the other very happily went to paradise with the Lord. Inward light and darkness, obedience and disobedience to God truly are as wide apart as heaven and earth.

At the same time the Lord enlightened me to know that my body was disobedient to the authority of God, and could not obey and was unable to, so before the presence of the Lord I asked for His mercy and light. After prayer I wrote what I saw in the following hymn:

(1) Lord Jesus, You are obedient. The Lord's obedience manifests my disobedience.

(2) The Lord's obedience has authority. The Lord's obedience dispels my disobedience.

(3) The Lord's obedience makes me obedient. The Lord has given me His obedience.

(4) The Lord's obedience is my obedience. The Lord's obedience becomes my obedience.

(5) The Lord's obedience lives within me. The Lord's obedience is immortal.

After this the Lord gave me to know I was to go and be a mother to orphans, and showed me a house for an orphanage at Zhenru. Despite this, I dared not move at all and dared not think; I only told this matter to Mrs David Chang. What I most feared all my life was to be a preacher and a mother. Now, not only did I *not* fear to be a preacher, but I hastened to do it – but to be a mother had been more difficult than I can describe. So I could only wait in the dark to see what leading and plan God had.

At times I had a crafty heart, fully hoping this call was only an illusion and not real. Every time these kinds of thoughts came, the voice of the inward call came with added clarity, showing that it had come from God. When I definitely knew the call came from God, inwardly I feared all the more. I truly feared the quarrelling and disturbance of children. In addition, I was old and strength was declining: how could I shoulder this heavy responsibility? I trembled with fear and did not know how it could be well. I could only put the matter down straight away and could not take it up.

I delayed until May 1942, when a voice in my heart urged me, and I had no alternative but to tell the matter to a brother in the Lord. He said, 'Since the Lord has called, please go to Zhenru and prepare.' I was truly mystified. Before long I also told this matter to my eldest son, and he had nothing for or against it. After this I asked for a proof from God, saying, 'For me to manage an orphanage, the first necessity is money. Please, Lord, give me a generous gift to manifest clearly that this matter is coming from You and that I can begin to prepare.'

My fourth son had sent to me from Hong Kong a military cheque for $100. I said to the Lord that this amount was too small and could not do anything. Then, the next day, suddenly I had a thought to go to a certain brother's home to see his wife. As soon as I arrived at his home our brother said, 'It is very good that you have come. I have a sum of money, $9,000, and I didn't know to whom I should give it. Now that you have come, I know inwardly that I should give it to you.'

I was silent. On the one hand, it was very clear that God's proof had come. On the other hand, I feared that I was not the one to manage this matter, and that I could not undertake this kind of work. I feared almost to trembling, torn to and fro between two difficulties.

On the 14th day another brother gave me $400. On the 17th June, on the morning I moved, my eldest son gave me $1,000 (he had never given me a gift like this before). Who would dare say this is not God's proof? I also talked over this matter with Miss Ruth Li, and what she said helped me to see God's will all the more clearly.

The Japanese occupation brought a big change in local

currency, and the sums of money mentioned for the orphanage were just about half their former value. She (Miss Ruth Li) said, 'Since God has called you out in old age to be a mother to orphans, it is certainly not to manage a charitable organisation, because a charitable organisation needs youth and vigour to be able to manage a lot of troublesome workers and be equal to the duties of the office. Since God wants you in old age to come out and be a mother to orphans, it is certainly on the spiritual side. Let other people manage the charitable business. You should only serve orphans of the children of the family of God, and stand together with us in one testimony.' When she spoke like this, inwardly I felt that I thoroughly understood. Oh my God! When Your words are explained, light is shed forth, causing the simple to understand.

On the morning of the 17th June 1942, Mrs David Chang took me to Zhenru to live temporarily at Gesan farm business centre. Two weeks later I moved to live at the orphanage. To begin with the house was repaired, and everything prepared. In everything I see God's grace and presence. As long as this elderly widow has still one breath on this earth, I wish to sing daily, 'The Lord's will be done.' A hymn I constantly sing is, 'My God, my Father . . . Thy will be done.'

The first sister who came to work with me, Mrs Joseph Huang, brought a girl orphan with her on the 25th August. That evening the brethren laid hands on her and dedicated her to the Lord. On the 7th September a second sister also came as co-worker, Miss Jiang Qingxin. The two sisters were truly sent of the Lord. Although the Lord God had not given us a woman servant, He gave us strength and unity, and, trusting in Him, everything was carried through. Before long Mrs Joseph Huang returned home, and God sent sister Chen Chongxin to work together with us here.

On the 18th October, brothers Yu Chenghua (Dr Yu) and Tang Shaolin came together to Zhenru to interview me, and were overcome with pleasure. I then told brother Yu how the orphanage had been established. He said that when Mr Müller had his orphanage he briefly recorded in his circulars most of the experiences that God had wrought with him. It would be good if I also briefly recorded what God had done for me. That same day I placed this matter before the orphanage brethren workers. They nodded in assent. So I have left the origin of this orphanage and God's call, leading and experiences here on record.

In March 1943, when I saw that Gesan farm was definitely to be sold, I lifted up my face to God and asked Him, saying, 'What, after all, should we do? Most of the utensils at the Faith Orphanage that I manage were borrowed from the farm.' God quickly gave me to see that they should all be restored to the farm, lest outsiders should come and remove things that belonged to the orphanage and dishonour the name of the Lord. On the 25th April the Lord also told me that the farm's tithe, which was fixed to be given to the orphanage, was to be entirely refused, because the Lord wanted my faith to be in God, not in the farm.

By the grace of God I make known God's correction about the farm, and because of this I am particularly happy. I have truly tasted much more of the compassionate joy of trust and obedience. Besides this, the Lord also gave me

grace to alter a few words in hymn no. 132, changing what
it speaks of to my own pathway:

> If the path I travel
> Leads me to the cross,
> If the way Thou choosest
> Leads to pain and loss,
> Let the compensation
> Daily, hourly, be
> Shadowless communion,
> Blessed Lord, with Thee.
>
> If there's loss of earth-joy,
> Give, Lord, more of heaven.
> Let the spirit praise Thee,
> Though the heart be riven:
> If sweet earthly ties, Lord,
> Break at Thy decree,
> Let the tie that binds us
> Closer, sweeter, be.
>
> Lonely though the pathway,
> Cheer it with Thy smile.
> Be Thou my companion,
> Through earth's little while;
> Selfless may I live, Lord,
> By Thy grace to be
> Just a cleansed channel,
> For Thy life through me.
> (M. E. Barber)

After this God's grace and blessings to me were truly many,
such as pen and ink cannot sufficiently declare.

The above is only a rough outline. May God Himself work in the reader's heart and bless. Amen.

April 1943
Ni Lin Heping

Against the Tide

by Angus Kinnear

Nee stood against the tide of Chinese Marxist atheism and Communism in the first half of the twentieth century. With millions of his books sold, studied and quoted in many languages, the most notable being *The Normal Christian Life*, he must surely be among the strongest influences on modern Christian thinking.

Once described as 'The most dangerous man in China', Watchman Nee was imprisoned for his faith, sentenced to 20 years' hard labour, brainwashing and physical torture. It is almost certain that in all that time he was not allowed a Bible.

When he died, a piece of paper was found beneath his pillow with several lines in large letters: 'Christ is the Son of God. He died as the Redeemer for human beings and was raised up from the dead after three days. This is the biggest thing in the universe. I shall die for believing in Christ.'

Nee once observed following a severe trial of faith: 'To keep our hand to the plough while wiping away our tears – that is Christianity.' Yet he was able to testify in his last letter before his death to the joy that was still in his heart.

Let this astonishing biography fill you with joy and faith in Christ, and transform your life and commitment to Him.

www.kingsway.co.uk